COOPERATION IN THE CLASSROOM
The Jigsaw Method

ELLIOT ARONSON

Elliot Aronson's primary research interests reside in the general area of social influence. Throughout his career he has tried to do experiments that would integrate his passion about basic science with his desire to apply these research findings toward improving the human condition (e.g., to reduce prejudice, deter bullying, and convince people to conserve energy and other natural resources).

Professor Aronson is the only psychologist to have won APA's highest awards in all three major academic categories: For distinguished writing (1973), for distinguished teaching (1980), and for distinguished research (1999). In 2002, he was listed among the 100 most eminent psychologists of the 20th Century (APA Monitor, July/August, 2002). In 2007, he received the William James Award for Distinguished Research from the Association for Psychological Science.

He has taught at Harvard University, the University of Minnesota, the University of Texas, the University of California at Santa Cruz, and Stanford University and is the author of many books, including *The Social Animal*, *Mistakes were made (but not by me)* (with Carol Tavris) and his recent autobiography *Not by Chance Alone*.

He lives in Santa Cruz, California, with Vera, his wife of more than 55 years.

COOPERATION IN THE CLASSROOM
The Jigsaw Method

ELLIOT ARONSON AND **SHELLEY PATNOE**

Cooperation in the Classroom: The Jigsaw Method
First published by Sage, 1978, under the title The Jigsaw Classroom
Second edition first published by Addison-Wesley Educational Publishers Inc. 1997
This edition published by Pinter & Martin Ltd 2011

ISBN 978-1905177-22-6 (paperback)
ISBN 978-1905177-79-0 (ebook)

British Library Cataloguing-in-Publication Data
A catalogue record for this book is available from the British Library

Printed and bound in the UK by
Martins the Printers, Berwick upon Tweed

Pinter & Martin Ltd
6 Effra Parade
London SW2 1PS
www.pinterandmartin.com

CONTENTS

FOREWORD

For many years, our educational system has been suffering from blind faith in such romantic notions as thinking that all children can become academically proficient (with not a one left behind!) just by passing laws that force schools to try harder. Or the equally "romantic" delusion that teaching abstinence to teenagers curbs premarital sex, despite years of data that just keep saying no. This sort of romanticism is destructive. But in its nondelusional form, educational romanticism can be a force for good and a wellspring for good science. I know this because my father is Elliot Aronson. I became aware of psychology during the stretch of my father's career when he began doing fewer of his laboratory experiments to test theory and more field experiments to test theory and improve human behavior. To have been introduced to psychology by this particular body of work and by my father was to learn at an early age that a great scientist can also be a great romantic, so long as he's as enamored of the truth as he is of good news.

My father's scientific disposition is the result, I believe, of the fact that he was the child of two great but parallel traditions in psychology, epitomized by his two significant mentors, Abraham Maslow and Leon Festinger. Whereas the softhearted Maslow modeled an exuberant faith in man's potential for growth and "self-actualization," Festinger, the hardheaded experimentalist, ingrained in him an equally strong zeal for scientific rigor, and an abiding impatience with sloppy thinking, imprecise operationalizations, and correlation coefficients. Years of exposure to this combination of scientist and humanist in my father have left me with a deep-seated optimism about the possibilities of education, if done right. Call it educational romanticism if you like. Behavioral geneticists tell me that, like all traits, the traits that make my father such a uniquely terrific scientist are heritable, and that they will increasingly manifest in me as I age. I hope so. I will never know, because scientific talent and integrity, coupled with optimism about human growth were so impeccably modeled by both my parents that nature and nurture are hopelessly muddled; both undoubtedly shaped my experiences as a son, a student, a father, teacher, and researcher.

Many years ago, a middle-aged scientist visited a school near his home to observe a group of children who, without knowing it, were subjects in an important social experiment. Young, Black, and uneducated, the children had been picked at random from the community to receive schooling, mainly in the form of Bible study, spelling, and, for the girls, household skills like embroidery. The premise of the experiment was to see whether the children could be educated and Christianized, and whether this could be done without provoking a backlash from members of the white community who opposed educating black people. The scientist's wife was first to see the experiment unfold, and she returned so enchanted with the children that she urged her husband see for himself.

When he went to the school he had quite the same reaction as his wife, but he also had a special epiphany of his own. He wrote to the director of the society that created the school to report being "much pleased" by his visit and to confess the unexpected effect of what he had seen:

> I have conceived a higher opinion of the natural capacities of the black race than I had ever before entertained. Their apprehension seems as quick, their memory as strong, and their docility in every respect equal to that of white children.

That was Benjamin Franklin writing in 1763. It is unfortunate that he never followed up on this experiment; American racial attitudes might have evolved more quickly had the country's premier scientist and celebrity replicated his experiment and convinced others that blacks were the intellectual equals of whites. The Philadelphia school and others like it closed down at the start of the revolution, and Franklin became too consumed with other matters to turn an experiment in Christian philanthropy into a program of research on race and intelligence. But clearly something happened in that school to create conditions that allowed a keen observer to glimpse in those children the innate intelligence hidden by the conditions of their everyday life as slaves.

To be sure, the school experiment was imperfect. For one thing, there was no formal control group of average white children; that group existed only as a simulation in Franklin's head. Nonetheless, it was persuasive enough a demonstration to change Franklin's mind for good.

For instance, 12 years earlier in his role as demographer, Franklin had written a report called Observations on the Increase of Mankind. In it he warned against a growing black population. "Why," he had asked, "increase the sons of Africa by planting them in America, where we have so fair an opportunity by excluding all blacks and Tawneys, of increasing the lovely white and Red?" His chief arguments echoed the genetic thinking of the times; black people were innately immoral, untrustworthy, and stupid. This attitude was most explicit in a line that read "almost every slave, being by nature a thief ..." That was in 1751.

In his 1769 revision of the report, published six years after his epiphany in the school, his change of heart shows up in an elegant stroke of editing: "Almost every slave," he wrote, "being from the nature of slavery a thief ..." Later still, in 1789, he wrote about the "Negro, who has long been treated as a brute animal, too frequently sinks beneath the common standard of the human species. The galling chains that bind his body, do also fetter his intellectual faculties, and impair the social affections of his heart."

Franklin thus became the first American, certainly the most famous, to recognize that the flaws of black people were rooted not in their inherent characteristics, but in their maltreatment—the first to convert from naturism to nurturism. He went on to become the most ardent abolitionist of the founding fathers.

In a scene that bears a striking resemblance to Ben Franklin's school visit two centuries earlier, in Texas in 1971 a young scientist named Elliot Aronson was summoned to observe schools near his home, this time by a perplexed former student, who was now the assistant superintendent for the Austin schools. Facing a crisis at work, the student found his mind drifting back to things he'd learned in my father's introductory social psychology course some years before. My father was a scientist who took teaching as seriously as laboratory work and publishing, and his courses became so popular that enrollment had to be determined by lottery. His lectures, stirring narratives about human nature, were based on hard science by social psychologists, but they were also infused with the softer side of psychology and the humanities—Sigmund Freud, Abraham Maslow, Edward Albee, Franz Kafka, Kurt Vonnegut, J. D. Salinger, and others—all woven into a passionate case for man's potential for both good and evil. In my father's class, students were introduced to the scary things that nice, ordinary people could do to one another under extreme circumstances. He showed a movie in which people delivered (apparently) fatal levels of shock to an innocent-looking man in the Milgram experiment and a nearly unbearable documentary about the horrors of Nazi Germany. There was also a movie in which a social psychologist with a funny beard rounded up nice and normal college students in their neighborhoods and locked them up in a mock prison in the psychology department with other nice and normal students acting as guards. In just a short time spent in this "Stanford Prison Experiment," their behavior degenerated to levels one might expect from real prisoners and real guards.

Yet my father argued that the ultimate message of these dark experiments—indeed the big message of social psychology—was an optimistic one. By understanding the power of the situation to corrupt human behavior, one could ultimately use this power for good. Get the situation right and people would treat one another better.

My father's former student reminded him of his lectures on the power of social psychology for doing good and challenged his former professor to prove it by helping him out. He and his colleagues were ordered to carry out the de-segregation plan mandated by the Supreme Court in the 1954 Brown v. Board of Education, the ruling that declared unconstitutional the practice of sepa-rate-but-equal schools for black and minority children. In Austin, as in much of the South, desegregation was not going well. Instead of yielding the hoped-for harmony, softening of racial prejudice, and improved learning and self-regard of minority students, the schools were descending into violence and chaos. Fights were commonplace, often bloody, and once in a while (among the students in junior high and high school) nearly fatal. Among these older students, an atmosphere of danger and apprehension had engulfed the class-rooms, the students' attention to learning largely subverted by the more press-ing goal of getting safely through the day. The Austin schools thus perfectly exemplified the disappointing results of desegregation efforts across the coun-try (e.g., Gerard, 1983; Gerard & Miller, 1975; Stephan, 1978).

It was not hard to comprehend the problem. Typically two years behind the white students in academic skills, the minority students were plucked from their neighborhoods to attend schools far on the other side of town. Each day they had to wake two hours before the white students to board buses to take them to the comparative splendor of Austin's west side. Sleepy and underpre-pared, they were dropped into this unfamiliar place to compete with students who were better off, better educated, and better rested, and who considered their new classmates to be—in every respect but physically—inferior. What's more, the predominantly white faculty didn't respect these newcomers either, didn't expect much of them, and didn't really want them there. Faced with this humiliation, many of the minority students disengaged during class; some be-came quiet and withdrawn, others unruly and loud. Between classes, they would frequently turn the tables—in the corridors, the cafeteria, the rest-rooms, or on the playgrounds, where street smarts and toughness reigned, and where there was strength in numbers. It was, simply put, a recipe for dis-aster. The superintendents were no fools: They could see all this. But what could they do about it?

The superintendent canceled school for a cooling off period, and when the schools reopened, my father and a group of graduate students came in to ob-serve. The research team fanned out in an elementary school and observed some fifth-grade classrooms, with my father's instruction to go in without pre-conceptions, "like visitors from Mars." What they saw was a troubling mirror image of the environment Ben Franklin had observed 200 years earlier:

> Observing the classrooms, it didn't take long for us to realize that the typical class-room was an intensely competitive, high stakes environment. The children were vying for the respect and even love of their teacher. There were clear winners and losers in these classrooms; there was an uneven playing field, and the black and Latino kids were guaranteed to lose. (J. Aronson, 2008)

The book before you tells you what happened next. My father devised an elegant intervention, a method of getting children to stop competing and excluding one another, to cooperate, to like one another, and, in so doing, to unleash the natural capacities of the minority students. The Jigsaw method was born.

Joshua Aronson

WHY WE WROTE THIS BOOK:
A FOREWORD (OF SORTS)
ABOUT A REVOLUTION (OF SORTS)

A quarter of a century ago, in concert with a few of my students and colleagues, I stumbled onto something that proved to be the beginning of a revolution of sorts. What we did was invent a teaching method—one that structured the educational experience for schoolchildren in such a way that they had no choice but to give up trying to beat each other and, instead, began to learn to cooperate.

I used the term "stumbled" in the preceding paragraph with full awareness. Ideally, we would like nothing better than to take credit for consciously participating in a revolution; but, in all honesty, that was never our intention. Indeed, it wasn't our intention even to invent a new teaching method. We entered the schools as social psychologists—as such, we were using our knowledge and skills to intervene in a difficult crisis—to find a way to reduce the interracial hostility and prejudice that had broken out in the Austin, Texas, school system in the aftermath of desegregation. In order to accomplish this task, we felt it was essential to diminish the competitiveness that seemed to be an integral part of the existing classroom atmosphere. This led us to try to get the students to cooperate with each other to achieve a common goal; accordingly, we invented a technique we called "the jigsaw classroom." It proved to be effective beyond our wildest dreams. Not only did the implementation of the jigsaw technique succeed in reducing hostility and prejudice among children, but it produced a wide range of other educational benefits as well.

What about the revolution? In 1971 (the year we entered our first classroom as social psychological researchers), cooperation among children in classrooms was virtually nonexistent. In 1981, only ten years later, John McConahay, a leading expert on race relations, called the impact of cooperative learning techniques on American education nothing short of a revolution—and designated the cooperative revolution as the single most effective practice for improving race relations in desegregated schools. And some five years later, the educational commentator Alfie Kohn estimated that over 25,000 teachers were now using some form of a structured cooperative learning method in the United States alone—and asserted that hundreds more were adopting it every year.

From the outset, it was always our intention to give this technique away to anyone who could possibly use it. Accordingly, this book is written primarily for teachers who are looking for ways to expand their classroom repertoire in a more cooperative direction. It is aimed at demonstrating the benefits of cooperative learning and showing teachers how they can easily adopt the jigsaw method and integrate it into their usual ways of teaching. We are enthusiastic about the method because it works; not only does it open the door to warmer, closer friendships within and across ethnic boundaries, it has also proved effective at raising the self-esteem of students while improving their performance and increasing their liking for school and their enthusiasm about learning.

Too good to be true? Perhaps—all innovations have their problems, and jigsaw is no exception; it is not a panacea. At the same time, we hasten to add that it has stood the test of time and has proven its effectiveness after some two decades of rigorous testing and evaluation by a great many talented researchers and teachers all over the world.

It gives me great pleasure to express my deepest appreciation to my earliest collaborators on this project—my colleagues and students at the time of discovery: Cookie Stephan, Nancy Blaney, Jev Sikes, and Mathew Snapp. Together, the five of us not only invented the jigsaw technique but also did much of the early systematic research demonstrating its effectiveness both in the public school classroom and in the social psychological laboratory. In 1978 the five of us also collaborated on *The Jigsaw Classroom,* a book that described the results of our early research. But, alas, old revolutionary texts never die, they just go out of print, a fate that has befallen our earlier book. Consequently, over the years, a great many teachers have asked how they could get their hands on a copy. I didn't know what to tell them.

The present volume is, in part, an answer to those requests; it borrows heavily from that earlier book and also reflects some of the thinking and research that followed. In those subsequent years, I had the benefit of collaborating with a host of very talented graduate students. These include Diane Bridgeman, Bob Geffner, Alex Gonzalez, Suzanne Yates, Erica Goode, Ruth Tebbets, Neal Osherow, Marti Gonzales, and Ruth Thibodeau. I am full of gratitude for their efforts and contribution to my thinking.

My coauthor on the present volume, Shelley Patnoe, is another former student of mine and present colleague. Dr. Patnoe is a uniquely talented social psychologist who wears several hats. She teaches social psychology at San Jose State University, and she is also a school psychologist practicing in the Campbell Union School District. It is largely through her unique contribution that the present volume exists and is focused on keeping the working teacher in mind—to make it as easily accessible and as useful in a school setting as possible. In this context, Dr. Patnoe wishes to express her special appreciation to Lori Loson for her help and her good example, and to Mark Cross, Dan West, Lorena Lowe, and the staff at Castlemont School, who have helped her appreciate, in countless important ways, why classroom teaching is such a good thing to do with one's life.

Finally, we would both like to thank all the elementary school teachers and their students, from coast to coast, who cooperated with us in our research and who served as subjects in our experiments; they proved to be a delightful and refreshingly critical group of colleagues. Specifically, thank you to the following reviewers: Deborah Butler, Wabash College; Jack Hassard, Georgia State University; Nancy Schniedewind, State University of New York at New Paltz; Patrick O'Brien, Kyrene de la Mirada Elementary School; Dan West, Alicia Elementary School; Marilyn Dadey-Cutrufo, Scales Elementary School.

Elliot Aronson

CHAPTER 1

CLASSROOM COMPETITION
AND CULTURAL DIVERSITY

American education has been in a state of crisis for almost as long as we can remember. This has been particularly true during the past four decades, when dramatic changes in our society as a whole have been reflected in our public schools, turning them into veritable pressure cookers. Added demands are being placed on teachers, who struggle to open minds and guide the development of skills in increasingly crowded and impoverished surroundings. Declining test scores have had many explanations: Teachers view many children as unprepared for learning when they first arrive at school. Parents point to the schools as incompetent to educate their children. Politicians blame "frills" and periodically demand that schools go back to basics. Everyone blames society for lowered standards of behavior. But finger pointing and blaming are not the best way to solve problems.

What is clear is that our society' is moving toward increased diversity, and children come to the classroom with almost as many different experiences and expectations as there are children. They have different personalities, different skills, different abilities, different cultural backgrounds, different levels of self-esteem, and different emotional needs. All of these must be accommodated—at least to some extent—in order for all children to learn efficiently. Most teachers are well aware that classroom learning is not an "either-or" proposition. Rather, a child's emotional well-being and sense of self are certain to have a powerful impact on his or her acquisition of traditional knowledge and basic skills in the classroom. Indeed, research has shown that, under conducive conditions, emotional and intellectual growth go hand in hand; sensible techniques aimed at increasing a child's emotional well-being also have a positive impact on learning the basics.

What are "conducive" conditions—and how can they be implemented? On the following pages we will describe one classroom technique that, over the past 25 years has succeeded in establishing a classroom atmosphere that produces positive changes in the performance, the morale, and the well-being of children. The technique is a very simple one; hundreds of teachers and thousands of students have mastered it quickly and enjoy using it. In a nutshell, the technique produces a classroom structure that enables children to cooperate with one another to attain their educational objectives and, simultaneously, to develop important interpersonal skills, and a sharp increase in mutual appreciation in an atmosphere that is exciting and challenging rather than threatening or anxiety-producing. As class sizes have continued to grow, teachers who have used this strategy have learned (to their delight) that they can rely, increasingly, on their students' enhanced interpersonal skills to help with classroom management. In the following chapters we will describe this technique and present some evidence for its efficacy. We will then present detailed ways of establishing it in the classroom. But first, let's take a brief look at the broader societal issues that form the background out of which this educational strategy emerged.

COMPETITION IN SOCIETY

Americans like to win. From the fans in sports arenas chanting 'We're number one" and the little leaguer who bursts into tears when his team loses to business leaders and economic pundits who worry about trade with Japan and the value of the dollar, our society asserts its allegiance to victory and its contempt for losers. Our economic system is based on competition and much of American life is framed in competitive terms; newspapers regularly publish rankings of everything from sports teams to movie box office receipts; magazines publish articles about the 50 most beautiful people, the 10 best restaurants, or the 25 Americans with the highest incomes. One of the worst things you can say about your neighbor is that he or she is "a loser"!

What are the consequences of this attitude? How do people behave when competition is a way of life? We experience a great deal of anxiety when our performance is being observed or measured; we come to view one another as competitors and potential enemies; we are forever looking over our shoulders lest someone overtake us. We may experience pangs of envy when an acquaintance lands a good job or becomes a successful doctor, lawyer, or barber and we come to look down on those who don't succeed. Once on this treadmill there is no respite, no resting place. For many people in our society, even reaching great heights of accomplishment leads not to peace but to still greater anxiety lest they fall from grace. And this anxiety is not unwarranted. Coaches who don't produce winning teams, salespeople who don't make quota, even scientists who don't publish first, find themselves looking for employment. In a society' obsessed with winning, each of us is only as good as our most recent performance. Some may become so anxious about losing that they decide to stop competing altogether; they become listless in school or at work, simply trying to get through the day—or they might drop out altogether.

This is not to suggest that competition is evil, or even that it is always dysfunctional. Under many circumstances, competition can be fun. It can add zest to an otherwise dull assignment. Moreover, there are situations where adding a dash of competition can enhance performance. But, over and over again, we have found that unbridled competition—the relentless concern with being number one, with beating the other person—can be, at best, limiting and, at worst, destructive and debilitating.

COMPETITION IN THE CLASSROOM

Intense competitiveness is not inborn, but, in our society, it often seems to be because it is learned so early and is so pervasive. Undoubtedly, for most of us, it is communicated and fostered by the family and the media. In the past, one of the major places where it was taught, indirectly but systematically, was in the classroom. Before looking at the competitive aspect of classroom education, it might be useful for readers to try to remember what it was like to be a youngster in elementary school. Some may recall their elementary school days with feelings of pleasant nostalgia, others with dread and anxiety. Either way, as all teachers know, it is almost invariably the bond (or lack thereof) with the teacher that stands at the center of the classroom experience. Recent innovations such as team teaching, computers in the classroom, and the extensive use of outside resources have added new dimensions to the atmosphere of many modern classrooms. But whether primarily traditional or primarily innovative, virtually all classrooms share two common aspects: (1) the major "process" that occurs is highly competitive, and (2) the ultimate goal of the competition among students is to win the approval and respect of teachers—and perhaps even their love.

The teaching process as it relates to competition is well known. Here is a common scene: The teacher stands in front of the classroom and asks a question that the students are expected to answer. A few children strain in their seats and wave their hands in the teacher's face, seemingly eager to be called upon. Several other students sit quietly with their eyes averted as if trying to make themselves invisible. If the student who is called upon comes up with the right answer, the teacher smiles, nods her head, and goes on to the next question. That smile and nod are a great reward. Among the other eager students, however, the success of the fortunate student causes disappointment because now they will have no opportunity to show the teacher how smart and quick they are—until the next question. Other students remain still, hiding.

Throughout this process, students learn several things. The first is that there is one and only one expert in the classroom: the teacher. They also learn that there is one and only one correct answer to any question asked: the answer in the teacher's head. The task is to figure out what answer the teacher expects. The students also learn that the payoff comes from pleasing the teacher by showing how quick, smart, neat, clean, and well behaved they are. The child knows that this is one way to gain the respect and love of this powerful person, this powerful person who may then be kind to the child and tell his or her parents what a wonderful person the child is. Other children may opt out of the academic race and satisfy their need for attention in other, less desirable ways!

The academic process, then, is one of intense competition, a very competitive game in which the stakes are extremely high. In conducting workshops in all regions of the country, one of the most touching things we have discovered is that, most people—even those in their sixties and seventies—can recall the names and faces of their elementary school teachers. Elementary school was a vivid place where important and memorable things happened to all of us. It was a place where the stakes were high precisely because it was important to be liked and respected by the teacher— who, naturally enough, was usually one of the two or three most important people in our world.

It is precisely because the teacher is so important that the generally competitive atmosphere in the classroom takes on such a powerful aura. Suppose you are a fifth grader; the teacher asks a question—and you know the correct answer. You raise your hand; but the teacher calls on one of the other students. What do you suppose is going on in your heart and mind? Are you hoping that the student recites the correct answer? Possibly. But in our research we have found that it is far more likely that you will sit there praying that he or she comes up with the wrong answer so that you will still have a chance to gain the attention of the teacher and show him how smart you are.

Furthermore, given the competitive atmosphere, it is likely that those who fail when called upon or who do not even raise their hands will resent those who succeed. They become envious, or try to denigrate more successful students by branding them "nerds" and they might find excuses to mock them or taunt them during recess. Or more likely, they may tune out altogether. The successful students, for their part, often hold the unsuccessful students in contempt, considering them to be dumb, uninteresting, not worth knowing. The result is that, to a greater or lesser extent, the competitive process when it takes place in an elementary school classroom is virtually guaranteed not to promote friendliness, understanding, and cooperation among students. Quite the reverse.

DESEGREGATION AND COMPETITION:
THE ORIGINS OF JIGSAW

In 1971, an exciting event took place in Austin, Texas. In accordance with the Supreme Court ruling of 1954, the public schools were desegregated. Unfortunately, as in many communities, this event did not occur without turmoil. Because Austin was residentially segregated at that time, the desegregation of the schools was implemented by means of a busing program. Thus, for the first time in their lives, youngsters from various ethnic and racial groups suddenly found themselves in close daily contact with one another. There was a great deal of conflict across racial lines, which occasionally flared into physical violence.

As it happened, Elliot Aronson, one of the authors of this book, was living in Austin (teaching at the University of Texas) at the time. As a social psychologist, Aronson had done a great deal of research in interpersonal relations. Moreover, as a father with four children in the public school system, he took more than a passing interest in the turmoil in the schools. As an experienced professional in crisis management, he considered several possible intervention strategies that might help in the immediate crisis, but he was much more interested in long-term prevention than in immediate alleviation of the symptoms. Let us explain.

Often when there is a "hot" crisis in the schools—with students engaging in interethnic conflict and aggression, the obvious short-term solution is to slap on a band-aid—for example, by instituting emergency multiethnic human relations councils that can begin discussing issues, problems, points of tension, and so forth. While this may be adequate as crisis intervention, it would be far better for the community if methods could be devised to *prevent* these tensions from developing. Moreover, it would be far more efficient and effective if these methods could be built into the structure of the institution rather than stitched on as an afterthought. Specifically, *it would be valuable if the basic process could be changed so that youngsters could learn to like and trust each other—not as an extracurricular activity but in the course of learning their reading, writing, and arithmetic.* In order to accomplish this goal, it might be useful to deal with students who had not been completely indoctrinated into the existing competitive process and had not yet developed deep-seated distrust for people of different racial and ethnic groups. For this reason, Aronson and his colleagues approached the situation as a learning problem, not as a crisis-management problem—and they began their research in the elementary schools rather than in the high schools.

THE PROBLEM

Before describing the resulting research, a word about the social psychology of desegregation. As you know, in 1954 in the landmark case of *Brown v. the Board of Education of Topeka, Kansas,* the Supreme Court declared that separate but equal schools were by nature unequal. This decision was based, in part, upon social psychological research which suggested that sending minority children to separate schools damages their self-esteem. The reasoning was that segregation implies that children from minority groups are inferior; thus there is no way that separate but equal schools can ever be equal, at least in spirit. That is to say, even if schools serving minority children were to have books and teachers and buildings of comparable quality to those serving the children of the establishment, they would still be by nature unequal because they would be separate, and being separated makes minority children feel inferior.

Recall that in those days, most social scientists believed that, as a direct result of this ruling, prejudice would be markedly decreased because increased contact among children of various racial groups would produce greater liking and understanding. Moreover, they had reason to believe that busing as a means of increasing interracial contact would not only increase mutual understanding but would also provide minority children with a richer educational experience. Indeed the monumental Coleman Report indicated that the exam performance of African-American children improved as the percentage of white children in their classrooms increased. But Coleman's data were based primarily on African-American children who were living in neighborhoods that were predominantly white. One began to suspect that these children might differ in many significant respects from children living in impoverished inner city neighborhoods.

And, sure enough, subsequent research in the California public schools by Harold Gerard and Norman Miller showed that when busing was used to integrate schools, no such improvement in the performance of African-American children occurred. Moreover, several years later, when Walter Stephan reviewed dozens of studies done in the aftermath of desegregation, he found no clear evidence that desegregation increased selfesteem among minority students. Rather, in 25 percent of the studies, the self-esteem of minority children actually decreased.

For us, the crucial variable is not busing but what happens when children get *off the* bus—that is, what happens in the typical classroom. And, as we have indicated, it was our contention that the academic competitiveness that existed in the classroom was crucial—for it is not a process that encourages students to look benevolently and happily upon their classmates; it is not a process designed to increase understanding and interpersonal attraction even among people of the same racial or ethnic background. Rather, the process induces competitiveness, one-upmanship, jealousy, and suspicion. When one adds to this situation the already existing racial tensions that were then and are still present in our increasingly multicultural society, it is little wonder that turmoil and even violence is frequently the result.

Moreover, the situation is even more volatile than we have pictured it. In most American cities, when schools were first desegregated students were competing with each other on unequal ground. Prior to 1954, the law of the land was "separate but equal." Unfortunately, there was plenty of separation, but very little equality. That is, schools in the neighborhoods that housed most ethnic minorities were not providing the same quality of education that was being offered in most middle-class white neighborhoods. Consequently, in Austin, for example, just prior to busing, the knowledge, reading skills, intellectual curiosity, and ability to compete in cognitive skills of most minority-group youngsters was inferior to that of their more privileged counterparts. And, as we all know, this inequality still exists. Specifically, in most communities today there are impoverished neighborhoods from which some of the neediest and least prepared students emerge, taxing severely the resources of the neighborhood school. Existing conditions can frustrate even the most gifted teacher.

Today, integration issues are even more complex. Instead of students bused from across town, teachers are now being asked to welcome into their crowded classrooms, immigrant children from dozens of nations, some of whom have had little schooling and speak no English. Other students are the children of economic refugees with a history of frequent moves and family environments that make education a low priority. The skills these children bring to school equip them for survival in a world very different from the one the school culture assumes. Teachers are also being asked to provide appropriate education for children with assorted learning difficulties and to include into their classrooms disabled students who were once educated in separate facilities. At the very least, these students are also likely to experience increased anxiety and low self-esteem when entering an educational environment for which they are not prepared.

Needless to say, we no longer believe that the simple act of inclusion is in itself a panacea. We are convinced that it is a necessary *first step* toward helping children accept and respect one another as individuals. But it is only the first step. It is clear that attention to the classroom process itself is vitally important.

Returning now to the Austin project, if our understanding of the process was correct, it was necessary to find a way to change the process— that is, to change the atmosphere in the classroom so that the children would no longer be competing against each other but would begin to treat each other as resources. Further, if our reasoning was correct, changing the process could have a beneficial effect upon the interpersonal relations of all students, not simply minority-group members. Recall that in the process we described, there was only one human resource in the classroom: the teacher, the source of all answers and virtually all rewards. In that process there is no payoff for consulting and collaborating with classmates. They are your enemies, your competitors; they, too, are trying to impress the teacher and get that attention and approval you want. Indeed, students who try to use the others as resources in the typical classroom may be reprimanded. Thus, not only is the process highly competitive and destructive to interpersonal relations—which is itself a heavy cost—but, in addition, a potentially valuable pool of human resources in the classroom is out of bounds.

THE JIGSAW CLASSROOM

The attempt in Austin to change the process was a relatively simple one employing a synthesis of principles gleaned from Aronsons years of work on small-group dynamics and social interaction. First, Aronson and his colleagues changed the basic structure of one expert (the teacher) and 30 listeners. This was accomplished by placing the students in small groups of five or six students each and changing the role of the teacher so that he or she was no longer the major resource for each of the learning groups. *This process made it imperative that the children treat each other as resources.* This was achieved in three ways:

1. The learning process was structured so that individual competitiveness was incompatible with success.
2. Success could occur only after there was cooperative behavior among the students in a group.
3. All students (no matter what their prior status in the classroom) were in a position to bring to their groupmates a unique gift of knowledge—a piece of vital information that was not readily available except from that individual student.

As mentioned earlier, the students in a traditional classroom are often rewarded when they succeed in attracting the teacher's attention by outshining their competitors. In the cooperative classroom, the students achieve success as a consequence of paying attention to their peers, asking good questions, helping each other, teaching each other, and helping each other teach.

How does this come about? An example will clarify. In the initial experiment, Aronson and his colleagues entered a fifth-grade classroom where the students were studying biographies of great Americans. The upcoming lesson happened to be a biography of Joseph Pulitzer.[1] The researchers created a biography of Joseph Pulitzer that consisted of six paragraphs. The first paragraph was about Pulitzers ancestors and how they came to this country; the second described his childhood and growing-up years; the third covered Pulitzer as a young man, his education, and his early employment; the fourth told of his middle-age years and how he founded his newspaper; and so forth. Each major aspect of Pulitzer's life was contained in a separate paragraph.

The researchers copied the biography, cut it into six one-paragraph sections and gave each child in the six-person learning group one of the paragraphs. Thus each learning group had within it the entire biography of Joseph Pulitzer, but each child had no more than one-sixth of the story. In order to learn about Pulitzer, the students had to master their paragraph and teach it to the others in their group. For example, David was responsible for Pulitzer as a young man, Geoff for Pulitzer as a child, and so forth. Each student took his paragraph, read it over a few times, and then joined his counterparts from the other groups. That is, David, who had Pulitzer as a young man, consulted with Geoff, Christy, Lori, and Jon, who had also been given the same paragraph to learn for their groups. They could use each other to rehearse and to be sure they understood the important aspect of that phase of Pulitzers life. In this way, each student became an expert in his or her segment of Joseph Pulitzer's life. We call these temporary groupings "expert groups."

This part of the process is of great importance in that it provides time, space and practice for the less articulate and less skillful students to learn the material and affords them an opportunity to make use of the more adept students as models for organizing and presenting their report. The mediation of the expert group helps to make the jigsaw experience virtually foolproof. As psychologist Roger Brown has pointed out, if it weren't for the expert groups, the jigsaw method might backfire. Brown likens the jigsaw experience to playing little League baseball: If the boy playing right field keeps dropping fly balls, it hurts the team and you might begin to get a little annoyed at him. By analogy; suppose you are dependent on the performance of a Hispanic youngster who is less than perfectly adept in English, and he is having some difficulty articulating his segment of the lesson. You might resent him. The expert groups provide all students with the opportunity to get a clear idea of how to present

---

[1] A wide variety of subject matter can be adapted for use with the jigsaw format. On the whole, narrative material that emphasizes reading and comprehension skills is the easiest to work with in groups. Because of this, we began with the area of social studies—including history, civics, geography and so forth—believing it to be the most naturally suited to the technique. The major skills required are reading and comprehension. However, jigsaw has been successfully used in teaching science, math, and language arts. In Chapter 4 we discuss the components of the jigsaw method.

the material—regardless of prior inequities in skill or preparation.

After spending ten or fifteen minutes in their expert groups, the children went back to their original jigsaw groups, where they were informed that they had a certain amount of time to teach their information to each other. They were also told that, at the end of that time (or soon thereafter) each student would be tested on his or her individual knowledge of Pulitzer's *entire* life. Clearly the students had to depend on one another to learn all their material. The process is highly reminiscent of a jigsaw puzzle, with each student possessing a single vital piece of the big picture. Because of this resemblance, the system came to be referred to as the "jigsaw" model.

When left to their own resources in such a structured situation, the children eventually learned to teach and to listen to each other, and they began to learn two important lessons:

1. None of them could do well without the aid of every other person in that group.
2. Each member had a unique and essential contribution to make.

Suppose you and I are in the same group. You have been dealt Joseph Pulitzer as a young man; I have Pulitzer as an old man. The only way that I can learn about Pulitzer as a young man is if I pay close attention to what you are saying. You are a very important resource for me. The teacher is no longer the sole resource; indeed, she is not even in the group. Instead, every kid in the circle becomes important to me. I do well if I pay attention to other kids; I do poorly if I don't. It's a whole new ball game.

A jigsaw classroom is not a loose, "anything goes" situation. It is highly structured. Interdependence is required. *It is the element of "required" interdependence among students that makes this a unique learning method, and it is this interdependence that encourages students to take an active part in their learning.* In becoming a teacher of sorts, each student becomes a valuable resource for the others. Learning from each other gradually diminishes the need to try to outperform each other because one student's learning enhances the performance of the other students instead of inhibiting it, as is usually the case in most competitive, teacher-oriented classrooms. Within this cooperative paradigm, the teacher learns to be a facilitating resource person, and shares in the learning and teaching process with the students instead of being the sole resource. Rather than lecturing to the students, the teacher facilitates their mutual learning, in that all students are required to be active participants and to be responsible for what they learn.

Cooperative behavior does not happen all at once. It requires time and practice for children to use this technique effectively because it is not easy to break old habits. In Austin, for example, the children had grown accustomed to competing during their first four years in school; accordingly, for the first several days of jigsaw, the students tried to find a way to compete, even though competitiveness was useless—and even dysfunctional. This concept is best illustrated with an actual example, which is typical of the way the children stumbled toward the learning of the cooperative process.

CARLOS: A CASE STUDY

In one of our groups there was a boy whom we will call Carlos. Carlos was not very articulate in English because it was his second language. He had learned over the years to keep quiet in the classroom because, frequently, when he had spoken up he had been ridiculed by some of his classmates. In the jigsaw method, Carlos was assigned Joseph Pulitzer's middle years. When it was his turn to communicate his paragraph to the other students, he had a great deal of trouble and was very uncomfortable about it. The Jigsaw method is not magic; indeed, as Carlos later told us, early on he actually liked the traditional way better. This is not surprising; in the system we had introduced, Carlos was forced to speak, whereas earlier he could avoid discomfort simply by remaining quiet.

The existing situation was even more complex. It might even be said that the teacher and Carlos had entered into a kind of implicit conspiracy: During the first few weeks of school, the teacher had gradually learned not to call on Carlos because when she did he would stumble, stammer, and fall into an embarrassed silence, and some of the other children would make fun of him. Her decision undoubtedly came from the kindest of intentions—she simply did not want to humiliate him. But, unfortunately, by ignoring him, she had, in effect, written him off, which reinforced his counterproductive behavior. In addition, the teachers attitude implied that Carlos was not worth bothering with—and this message was unintentionally conveyed to the other children in the classroom. Children notice things and draw their own conclusions; they came to believe that there was one good reason why the teacher was not calling on Carlos: She felt he wasn't smart enough. Indeed, it is likely that even Carlos himself began to draw this conclusion. When one looks at the dynamics of that situation, it is no wonder that research had shown that desegregation often resulted in a further decrease in the self-esteem of underprivileged minority[7] children.

Let's go back to our six-person group. Carlos had to report on Joseph Pulitzer's middle years and was having a very hard time. He stammered, hesitated, and fidgeted. The other children were not very helpful; they had grown accustomed to a competitive process and responded out of this old, overlearned habit. They knew perfectly well what to do when a rival stumbles—

especially one from a different ethnic group whom they believe to be stupid. They ridiculed him, put him down, teased him. During our experiment, a couple of the youngsters in Carlos's group said such things as "Aw, you don't know the answer," "You're dumb," and "You don't know what you're doing."

In our first experiment, the groups were being loosely monitored by a research assistant who was moving from group to group. Observing this situation, our assistant intervened by saying something like: "O.K., you can say things like that if you want to; it might be fun for you, but it's *not* going to help you learn about Joseph Pulitzer's middle years, and you will be having an exam on Pulitzer's life in about 20 minutes."

Notice how the reinforcement contingencies have shifted! No longer do the children gain much from putting Carlos down; now they stand to lose a great deal. After a few days and several similar experiences, it began to dawn on the children that the *only* way they were going to learn about Pulitzer's middle years was by paying attention to what Carlos had to say. Out of necessity they gradually began to develop into pretty good interviewers. If Carlos was having a little trouble communicating what he knew, instead of ignoring him or ridiculing him, they began to ask probing questions. They became junior versions of Barbara Walters or Charlie Rose, asking the kinds of questions that made it easier for Carlos to communicate what he was thinking. Carlos began to respond to this treatment by becoming more relaxed, and as he relaxed his ability[7] to communicate improved. After a couple of weeks, the other children realized that Carlos was not dumb, as they had originally thought, and began to respect him, open up to him, like him. Carlos began to enjoy school more and began to see the Anglo kids in his group not as show-offs and tormentors but as helpful and responsive. He began to like them.

BASIC RESULTS

What happened in Carlos's group is a good example of the jigsaw technique and how it frequently worked to produce beneficial effects, but it hardly constitutes acceptable scientific data. For that, we must turn to the field experiments performed by Aronson and his colleagues in Texas and California in which the effects of the jigsaw techniques on interpersonal attraction, self-esteem, and happiness in school were investigated systematically. Initially, in Austin, the jigsaw technique was instituted in several classrooms for six weeks and assessed for its effectiveness by taking measures at the beginning and end of the period—comparing the performance of the children in the jigsaw classrooms with the performance of children in more traditional, competitive classrooms being taught by some of the most effective teachers in the school system.

This research will be described in detail later but as a preview we will tell you that the major findings were quite consistent:

1. Children in the jigsaw classrooms grew to like their groupmates even more than they liked others in their classroom.
2. Children in the jigsaw classrooms liked school better (or, at least, hated school less) than their counterparts in competitive classrooms. Absenteeism among jigsaw students decreased dramatically.
3. The self-esteem of the children in the jigsaw classrooms increased to a greater extent than that of children in competitive classrooms.
4. In terms of the mastery of classroom material, children in the jigsaw classrooms outperformed children in competitive classrooms. This difference was primarily due to improvement in the performance of underprivileged minority students; specifically, although white children performed as well in either type of classroom, African-American and Latino children performed significantly better in jigsaw classrooms than in competitive classrooms.
5. As a result of their experience in jigsaw groups, children learned to empathize with one another; that is, compared to children in traditional classrooms they found it easier to put themselves in another person's shoes and experience the world as if they were that other person.

These basic results have been replicated and extended in several school districts in different parts of the country.

WHY USE JIGSAW

While the jigsaw technique was developed as an attempt to bridge the gap between children from different ethnic groups, these results make clear that its function is not limited to multiracial situations. In any classroom situation, the jigsaw method curbs some of the undesirable aspects of excessive competition and increases the interest children have in cooperating with one another. Thus the research demonstrated that what seemed to be a deeply ingrained kind of behavior—competitiveness—can be modified.

Our aim is not to eliminate a child's ability to compete; a certain amount of competition can be fun and may, in many circumstances, enhance performance without producing negative consequences. *What we want to do is teach cooperativeness as a skill.* This means that when individuals find themselves in situations where cooperativeness is the most productive strategy they will not view everyone in sight as competitors and doggedly try to defeat them.

Also, cooperative learning in general, and the jigsaw method in particular, can be a useful addition to individualized learning programs. When individualized instruction utilizes independent study, it frequently results in reducing the child's opportunity to develop social skills in the learning environment. Complementing individualized instruction and other classroom experiences with cooperative groups could provide a beneficial balance as well as an interesting set of experiences. In this context, it should be noted that the children in these experiments were exposed to the jigsaw technique for only a small fraction of their time in school—often as little as three or four hours per week. The rest of the time they were learning in a generally competitive atmosphere. These results show that children can learn the skills of cooperation and that cooperative activities can have an important and beneficial effect on their lives, even when these activities are presented in a basically competitive atmosphere. This is encouraging because it means that parents and teachers do not need to choose between cooperation and competition; both can occur in the same classroom. Moreover, by working in jigsaw groups, the children learned that *it is possible to work together in a helpful way without sacrificing excellence* and that working together increases their positive feelings about themselves and their happiness in school. Finally, it is our contention that experiencing cooperativeness will increase tolerance for temporary failure both in others and in ourselves; our hope is that this technique can lead to a reduction in the anxiety that is too frequently associated with performance in our society.

CHAPTER 2

COOPERATIVE LEARNING: BACKGROUND AND ISSUES

As most teachers now know, cooperative learning provides many benefits. Over the past few years, as new methods and strategies have been developed, cooperative group work has become a regular tool for learning in classrooms everywhere. In addition to improved social skills, other benefits include language development and critical thinking. And, as described previously, cooperative learning also allows systematic equal status interaction among students of varied linguistic and cultural backgrounds. All of these benefits are important in today's crowded multicultural classroom.

In the chapters that follow we will describe the jigsaw method in detail. But first we would like to provide an overview of some of the other methods now available.

COOPERATIVE LEARNING STRATEGIES

Cooperative learning is not simply a matter of putting students in groups and expecting them to learn. In fact, research has shown that when students are put together in groups but given little structure and few incentives, there are few if any positive effects on learning. More is needed. Over the past 25 years, a number of perspectives on cooperative learning methods have been developed. Research has been done, issues have been discussed, and techniques have been refined and there is now much to choose from. There seems little doubt that cooperative learning is useful for teachers. However, there are many questions to answer before deciding on an appropriate cooperative method for a given situation. Among the issues to be considered are the age and ability of the students, the subject matter to be studied, the structuring of tasks, the goal of the lesson, and the rewards to be offered. Pondering the answers to these questions will help a teacher select the most appropriate method for a particular situation. Here is a brief summary of some of those perspectives.

STRUCTURES FOR COOPERATIVE LEARNING

Spencer Kagan has developed a structural approach to cooperative learning. He conceptualizes a sequence of behaviors that can be developed in the classroom to "structure" classroom interaction. Included are dozens of ways to structure tasks, rewards, goals, resources, and roles—the tools needed to develop positive interdependence and also to shape learning experiences.

With these structures, Kagan offers a classroom process separate from content. Structures can be defined as the social organization of the classroom. When content is added, the result is what is called an activity. Lessons are made up of activities and since structures are content free, they can be used to deliver any curriculum.

The structures have different functions such as team-building or classbuilding, and there are structures appropriate for all ages. Many useful structures such as *heads together* or *think-pair-share* help young elementary school age children learn some of the component skills for cooperative learning. These skills are immediately useful and they can be developed later as the child matures. Other structures such as *numbered heads* and *Pairs check* are aimed at content mastery; still others such as "Value Lines" help develop communication skills.

STUDENT TEAM LEARNING METHODS

Robert Slavin has developed and researched an array of cooperative learning methods appropriate for a variety of subjects and situations. These methods motivate student achievement through the use of competition between groups and through individual and group recognition. His structures take into account such issues as the nature of the goals, both individual and group accountability, equal opportunity for success, motivation, and concern for individual needs. The methods he has developed are outlined here.

Student Teams Achievement Divisions (STAD)

In the STAD method, heterogeneous learning teams are assigned by the teacher. Students then study worksheets based on material presented by the teacher. Teams practice working problems together and studying together, but tests are taken individually. The resulting individual scores then contribute to an overall team score. In the interests of fairness, an individuals contribution to the team score is based on that person's improvement, not on his absolute score. This encourages each student to work because each contribution matters. Another motivator developed by Slavin is a weekly class newsletter that recognizes individual improvement and team performance.

Teams-Games-Tournaments (TGT)

TGT uses the same classroom format as STAD except that mastery is demonstrated through competition in a class tournament. This tournament is played between three similarly scoring students from different teams. Individual player scores contribute to their team score. Here again, a newsletter is used to help motivate students.

Jigsaw II

This is a modification of the jigsaw method that includes two important changes. First, all team members read the entire lesson to be learned rather than only one part. Second, as with Slavin's other methods, individual improvement scores combine to contribute to an overall team score. The rest is the same. As with the original jigsaw, students become experts on one aspect of the lesson, meet in expert groups, and help others in their group to learn the material. Success is measured through individual quizzes. Finally, a class newsletter recognizes individual improvement and team success.

Team Accelerated Instruction (TAI)

The TAI method of math instruction combines individual and team learning. Elementary school children work at their own level on math worksheets. Others in their group check the work with the help of answer sheets. This enables students to help each other even if they are working at a different level. Team rewards are based on individual productivity and accuracy.

Cooperative Integrated Reading and Composition (CIRC)

This is a program for reading and writing in late elementary school. Student pairs from two different reading groups work together on reading and writing tasks such as identifying main ideas, writing drafts, vocabulary, and spelling. As with TAI, students work with others, but at their own level. Again, team rewards are based on individual improvement scores.

LEARNING TOGETHER

David Johnson and Roger Johnson have developed a perspective on cooperative learning and a program of research to explore its effectiveness. They have been interested in the most effective way to structure learning in the classroom. In addition to the concerns about achievement examined by Robert

Slavin, they add concern with the effect of cooperative learning on social-emotional development and on group interaction.

Learning Together is a more conceptual approach than the two just mentioned. As Johnson and Johnson see it, learning successfully in groups depends on four components: (1) face-to-face interaction, (2) positive interdependence, (3) individual accountability, and (4) the development of interpersonal/group skills. Their contention is that the structure of social interdependence in a group determines how things turn out. Based on theorizing and research by Morton Deutsch, they note that interdependence can be both positive (cooperation) or negative (competition): You need someone else in order to cooperate or to compete. (They describe a third kind of connection, social dependence, in which you need another but that person doesn't need you e.g., a tutor or a coach.) Finally, there is independence or what they term "individualistic situations." They have explored the conditions under which cooperative, competitive, and individualistic efforts increase achievement, foster interpersonal relationships, and promote individual psychological well-being. They note that all are necessary in the classroom. Their interest is in the whole child, not just academic achievement.

GROUP INVESTIGATION

Shlomo Sharan developed a method known as group investigation, which combines independent, pair, and group work and offers a group reward for individual achievement. The teacher sets the problem for the class, but students choose what they want to study in order to explore an issue. The work is divided among the members of the group, who work individually, but the integration, summary, and presentation of findings are a group decision. It is a kind of advanced cooperative learning with the teacher's role being that of facilitating investigation and helping to maintain cooperative norms in the classroom. Group members cooperate to set learning goals, and they cooperate in planning how to find the means of reaching those goals. Finally, they collaborate with the teacher to evaluate their effort. Sharan points out that this is the way problems are solved in communities in the real world.

COOPERATIVE LEARNING: ISSUES

There have been literally hundreds of studies investigating cooperative learning. Researchers have asked whether cooperative learning increases academic achievement and if so under what conditions? Researchers have also asked if cooperative learning promotes social-emotional development and if so under what conditions. Other researchers have investigated the effect of cooperative learning on self-esteem, classroom climate, student liking for school, and the development of friendships. The following section summarizes some of the conclusions based on a series of meta analyses conducted by leading researchers in the field.

COOPERATIVE LEARNING AND ACADEMIC ACHIEVEMENT

An early (1980) analysis by Shlomo Sharan and Robert Slavin (1990) indicated that TGT/STAD may be more effective than other cooperative learning methods for basic skills acquisition. They concluded that the motivation for such achievement was the existence of extrinsic rewards, peer pressure, and inter-group competition. They also found that group investigation may foster development of higher-order thinking skills. Since group investigation involves group projects with problem-solving tasks chosen by the students, they concluded that the motivator in this case was intrinsic interest.

In 1981, Johnson, Johnson, and Maruyama conducted a meta-analysis of 122 studies of cooperative learning conducted between 1924 and 1981. They included *all* studies, no matter how flawed, and *all* methods, no matter how appropriate. They found that cooperative learning increased achievement and productivity in the classroom. Moreover, they followed up that analysis with an analysis including only well-designed studies and found even stronger support for the link between cooperative methods and academic achievement.

Robert Slavin responded in 1983 to Johnson, Johnson, and Maruyama analyses with a metanalysis of 46 studies. He included only well-designed studies that measured individual achievement as the outcome (eliminating the productivity variable that had been included in the Johnson and Johnson's analysis). Slavin's analysis addressed this question: Under what conditions does cooperative learning increase student achievement? He found that 89 *percent of the cooperative learning methods that included both individual accountability and group rewards found academic gains.* Overall, his results echoed those found in the early analysis: About two thirds of the studies showed positive effects on achievement and fewer than 5 percent showed negative effects.

In a 1990 meta-analysis that included 32 well-designed experiments of longer than three weeks, Slavin found increases in self-esteem. In this case, he defined self-esteem as achievement and being liked by others.

Also in 1990, Johnson and Johnson conducted an analysis of research reports comparing cooperative, competitive, and individualist goal structures. They found that simply interacting within an individualistic reward structure or being a member of a group is not enough for success. The key requirement is positive interdependence. That is, students must interact with and depend on one another for cooperative learning to be successful. They noted the same achievement and productivity gains that had been found before and added to those variables the finding that cooperative learning also benefits social relations and self-esteem.

COOPERATIVE LEARNING AND SOCIAL-EMOTIONAL GAINS: BASED ON THE RESEARCH, WHAT WORKS?

In a 1989 meta-analysis, the Johnsons again found strong support for the social benefit of cooperative methods. Their data were based on nearly 200 studies that looked at interpersonal attraction, more than 100 studies measuring social support, and about 80 studies on self-esteem benefits.

To summarize, then: According to Robert Slavin's analysis, the following methods are important for achievement gains using cooperative learning:

- Recognize or reward group success.
- Make individuals accountable; they should contribute to overall team score. (Avoid single team products.)
- Use gain scores: This allows students to contribute meaningfully to team success. This motivates weak students by leveling the playing field. And it motivates strong students to help weaker students out of self-interest; if the weaker student improves, the group score improves.

David and Roger Johnson concluded that the essential components of cooperation in the classroom are the following:

- Individual accountability: They see this as a necessary component of positive interdependence and promotion of individual responsibility.
- Face-to-face interaction: This helps students invest in the success of others, and it encourages cognitive elaboration.
- Use of interpersonal and group skills, including attention to the group process.

So, when it comes to *achievement* gains, there are two key variables:

- Individual accountability
- Group goals

Regarding *social-emotional* development, the same two variables matter most:

- Individual accountability
- Group goals

Three others are also important:

- Positive face-to-face interaction
- Direct instruction in the component interpersonal skills
- Instruction in group process skills

Individual Accountability   Individual accountability is a structural issue and can be built into a cooperative group in two ways: (1) scoring and (2) task specialization. Individual accountability can first be built in through contributing an individual score to an overall group score, as found in Slavin's methods. The Johnsons also offer a variety of scoring strategies. Individual accountability can also be built in through task specialization. That is, each individual has a unique contribution to make to the overall group product and this can be traced. Task specialization can be found in jigsaw and in group investigation.

Group Goals   The issue of group goals is a motivation issue. Social rewards such as recognition and praise by the teacher are always effective motivators. Also, individuals can be rewarded through grades and with recognition in the form certificates or other external rewards. But this is a decision that needs to be made by individual teachers, depending on where they stand on the intrinsic versus extrinsic motivation issue.

Groups can be rewarded in the same ways as individuals. However, if you have a group goal without individual accountability there is always the danger of social loafing. Assigning a single grade to a group or a group project means that you run the risk of students deciding that it would be strategic for the more able students to carry the academic load. This might improve the final product and the resulting grade but it sacrifices any social benefits that may accrue to the group interaction, to say nothing of the fact that the less able students may learn nothing. Here either individually identifiable contributions to a total group product or task specialization provide a solution: That is, the group cannot do well unless every group member contributes.

Positive Face-to-Face Interaction and the Development of Skills   The social-emotional benefits of cooperative learning require positive face-to-face interaction. This can be developed through training of students in social skills and in the use of group process principles. Students need systematic lessons in how to interact with one another in positive and respectful ways, and they need instruction and practice in how to communicate effectively. Group process skills, paying attention to others in the group and to how the group itself is working, also needs to be taught and practiced. But it is worth it. These are skills that are not only useful but necessary. As Shlomo Sharan noted about his group investigation method, which depends on the existence of these skills, this is how problems are really solved in the world.

WHERE DOES JIGSAW FIT IN?

Suppose you are a teacher and are interested in implementing cooperative learning strategies in the classroom. When would you want to use the jigsaw method in preference to any of the other techniques? We believe that the jigsaw method is easy to implement and works well with a wide range of students. We have seen special benefits flow from one special aspect of jigsaw: namely, that each team member enters the situation bearing a unique gift—a part of the lesson that is unattainable elsewhere. This immediately makes each participant a person to be valued by the others.

At the same time, there are situations where one of the other methods might be more effective. Responding to the questions mentioned earlier about the age and ability of students as well as the specific subject matter, we would suggest the following: Jigsaw is most powerful and appropriate in situations where learning is from text-based material—such as social studies, literature, or science—that can be divided equally among students. It thus stands to reason that in order for jigsaw to work well the majority of participating students must have fairly well-developed reading skills. Accordingly, we would not recommend jigsaw for very young children.

With text-based subjects, reasons, connections and sequences are often important; the sharing of such materials helps the development of cognitive elaboration and language skills and helps students learn to understand subjects from different perspectives. Moreover, discussing with others how best to communicate the material is an aid to critical thinking and helps practice problem solving. A certain level of cognitive development is required to gain these benefits from jigsaw. Thus, except in unusual circumstances, we would not recommend it prior to the fourth grade. But the upper range of student age and experience is virtually unlimited. College students and adults in workshop settings particularly enjoy the positive interaction provided by jigsaw[7].

If you are thinking of using cooperative learning for teaching arithmetic or spelling, which depend on the practice of (in some cases) rote skills and where correct answers can be shared with other students but without understanding or insight to support them, then another method might be more appropriate.

Success in a jigsaw group also depends on enlightened self-interest. *Although the reward structure is individual rather than group, positive interde-*

pendence is built in through task specialization because students need each other to "get the whole picture."

Finally, what about social development? By definition, all cooperative learning methods depend on interpersonal interaction. Most require a smooth group process in order to work successfully whether the goal is academic achievement or interpersonal development. However, most of the methods described above share with jigsaw many of the following components and requisite skills:

- Small heterogeneous groups, organized by the teacher
- Team-building
- Structured positive interdependence
- Individual accountability
- Social skill development
- Examination of group process
- Special roles

In the chapters that follow, we offer ideas, exercises, and solutions to help facilitate interpersonal interaction and group process in the classroom. Whether students are working independently, in pairs, or in groups, whether they are cooperating or competing with one another, there are basic interpersonal and communication skills that will help facilitate the process. These skills help not only with classroom management but also with the social-emotional development of young students, giving them a good foundation for civilized peer interaction during the difficult middle and high school years. For older students, the interpersonal interaction adds to the richness of their intellectual experience. The ideas and suggestions that follow are presented as part of the jigsaw method. However, what follows in this book can be useful for developing the skills required any time individuals need to work together.

CHAPTER 3

HOW TO TRANSFORM A COLLECTION OF COMPETITIVE INDIVIDUALS INTO A COOPERATIVE GROUP

No two people are exactly alike—thank goodness! And nowhere is that more in evidence than in the classrooms of our own country. We are a nation of immigrants—originating from all areas of the world—and we bring with us myriad experiences. Thus the typical American classroom is a collection of different personalities—each one shaped by different family and cultural environments; each student in school with his or her own needs, skills, attitudes, and techniques of surviving—if not excelling—in the school environment. A teacher in a jigsaw classroom will be able to use this diversity to the advantage of all children. But before this technique can function constructively, the students must acquire the ability to work with their classmates in a cooperative, supportive manner.

Cooperation is the crux of the jigsaw approach. Over a quarter of a century ago, when jigsaw was first invented, competitiveness was deeply ingrained in the structure of the typical American classroom. Today, partly through the impact of cooperative learning techniques, many of the component skills for cooperative interaction are being cultivated in schools everywhere. Indeed, in many schools, youngsters are being encouraged to work with their classmates from the time they enter kindergarten. In many schools, skills for social interaction and conflict resolution are currently being taught and nurtured both in the classroom and on the playground. Attention is being paid particularly to developing such skills as listening to others without interrupting, checking for correct understanding, treating others with respect, understanding how others feel, and controlling emotions.

By the time children are in the third or fourth grade, they may have already developed some emotional literacy and learned to recognize and respect differences in others. Or at least they have begun to learn some behaviors that "look as if" they had developed these qualities with real understanding yet to develop. These individual skills are important because many teachers use them as part of their classroom management technique. Nonetheless, children still need help in developing the ability to work effectively in groups. The ability to work together smoothly is particularly important with the jigsaw technique because the success of individual group members depends on learning from others. Let's now look at some techniques for developing useful positive interdependence in the classroom.

DEVELOPING A COOPERATIVE LEARNING ENVIRONMENT

At the beginning of the school year, it is too much to expect students with little preparation to know how to work together cooperatively on a difficult academic task. You are asking them to learn both the content and a new process at the same time, and probably neither will be mastered. The resulting frustration is apt to cause discouragement and boredom. Instead, teachers have found that jigsaw classes are more successful when students have a chance to work together through team-building exercises *before* the curriculum material is tackled in the jigsaw format. This serves to make the process familiar and comfortable before any content learning has to begin. A short period each day for one or two weeks is generally sufficient time for this team-building, and it is well worth it in the long run.

Although team-building exercises may be conducted with the class as a whole, they are usually done in small groups so students can experience the organization of their new learning environment from the beginning. To develop group cohesiveness, we usually assign students to their first jigsaw group and do the team-building within that group.[1]

Before we discuss the specifics of team-building, though, let's look at the composition of a typical jigsaw group.

Group Composition

The size of the jigsaw group may vary from three to seven students, with five or six an ideal size. The fewer the children in a group, the more limited their opportunity to learn how to work with a variety of people. On the other hand, in groups larger than six or seven, beyond the obvious problems with management, individual students do not seem to have enough chance to speak, and consequently their interest drops. However, in groups containing mem-

[1] Some teachers have found that beginning team-building in the format of a class meeting is helpful. With the entire class seated in a large circle, a simple interviewing exercise can be used. For example, in one exercise that teachers have found both useful and popular, students form pairs then interview each other: Who are YOU? Where do you live? What did you eat for breakfast? What do you like or dislike most about school? Then, on the basis of that information each student introduces his partner to the class. The class meeting format can be used to begin to teach some of the interpersonal skills needed for cooperative interaction such as listening, paying compliments, as well as providing an opportunity to practice such skills as solving problems without name-calling or "put downs."

bers who are chronically absent, it is sometimes wise to include an extra "redundant" member. This extra member can "shadow" the person likely to be absent or simply fill in for someone not there on a particular day—whatever works best in the situation, for the group and for the child.

Jigsaw teachers have found a diverse group of students is more desirable than a homogeneous one. Thus jigsaw groups should ideally contain both boys and girls, assertive and nonassertive students, fast and slow readers, and members of different racial or ethnic groups. Such diversity in the jigsaw group extends the potential learning resources available to each student. For example, the slow learner may be stimulated and helped by a more highly motivated student who is, in John Holt's phrase, "a competence model within reach." The slow learner in turn provides the quicker student with a valuable opportunity to acquire effective interpersonal and tutoring skills. Furthermore, exposure in jigsaw groups to children with different personalities and backgrounds is enriching in a way that can extend beyond the classroom. Jigsaw students are challenged to develop empathy and tolerance, and they must learn to work effectively toward common goals with persons differing from themselves in experience and capability. Increasingly, this latter skill is one that is needed in most occupations in the adult world, where there is a frequent demand for flexibility and the ability to work constructively with others in a group task or common goal.

We might say here that the "diversity is best" rule has its exceptions.

Placing best friends and worst enemies in the same group might provide a desired diversity of skills, but such combinations are best kept out of the same groups, at least in the beginning. Best friends tend to form a coalition, a sort of competing group within the group; the unresolved but powerful feelings of enemies obviously distract from the process goal of learning to cooperate. After students have some practice with jigsaw, existing personal relationships might not need to be an important consideration in composing groups. Indeed, a teacher may even decide that students who dislike each other, having learned some tolerance, or at least having learned to behave in a tolerant manner in other jigsaw groups, could now profit from being in the same group.

In some sense, every jigsaw group is an experiment based on the teacher's knowledge and intuition of what the students need and are capable of at any given point in their development. The duration of a group is also flexible. For example, at the start of a year, students may need to work together in the same group five or six weeks. Later, when their group skills have evolved more fully and they can adapt more readily to others, the teacher may want to change the groups every few weeks so that students have a chance to work with a greater variety of people.

OLDER STUDENTS

For students experienced with jigsaw, forming a group can be as simple as counting off heads. For example, if you want to form five heterogeneous groups of six students quickly, count off the students in the room, counting from one to six, five times. Then simply say, "All the ones meet here, all the twos over there" and so on. Latecomers and those absent at the time are simply added to groups as they arrive. This method is particularly effective with college students or in situations with adults who are not usually assigned seats but nonetheless tend to sit in the same general area of a room for an entire course. This affords the front-row sitters an opportunity to interact with the students who stay in the back and helps undermine the stereotypes each holds about the other. With older students, this mixing, even if it is for just a short time, adds measurably to the quality of overall class discussion. With the older students or younger students experienced with cooperative methods, a short warm-up or team-building exercise can help develop enough cohesiveness to begin a jigsaw project.

TEAM-BUILDING AND HELPING SKILLS

Imagine that you are a teacher and that your students are in small jigsaw groups for the first time. The more assertive children are excited and fidgety, ready for a new opportunity to prove themselves. Those children who tend to be shy may already be withdrawing under the pressure of changed circumstances. Your team-building goal is to give all students the experience of being valuable group members. Moreover, you want them to discover that for some tasks, a cooperative strategy is more effective than a competitive one. You want them to see that, for these tasks, competitive behavior both hinders the group and makes individual success impossible. The following team-building exercises can be used to facilitate the transition to cooperative learning. The short exercises were designed to make it easier for students to teach as well as to improve listening and helping skills. Here are some quick exercises you might use.

Learning to Listen Ask students to introduce themselves by name—all at the same time! Of course, no one will hear anyone else's name since they will all be talking at once. The merits of turn taking and listening to one another will be immediately obvious. The ensuing discussion will likely focus on the inability to listen while talking, thereby setting the scene for group agreement that listening would be a very important part of teaching and learning.

Group Picture   This exercise gives students useful practice in contributing to a common product. Have each group draw a group picture by passing paper and pen from person to person. Each student must add something to the picture as it circulates around the group several times. When the pictures are completed, discuss the importance of each members contribution. We have found that the discussion after the group-picture exercise invariably focuses upon the importance of each member's contribution. Students spontaneously express their belief that the groups work would be incomplete without everyone's full participation and that one person trying to dominate the activities necessarily resulted in one or more persons feeling left out. The group picture thus becomes a convenient vehicle for illustrating that working together rather than separately sometimes can be very useful.

The Broken Squares Game   This useful team-building game depends on nonverbal communication and helps students learn to observe others carefully rather than to think only about their own needs.

All group members receive three pieces of a puzzle. They are told that the object of the game is for each person to end up with a completed square. The pieces each person needs are distributed among teammates, so no group member is going to be able to complete the puzzle alone. Nor can group members simply take a needed piece from someone else. They can only give away one of their own pieces to help another group member complete his or her square. To encourage all members to be actively helpful to others instead of waiting to see who can help them, no communication is allowed. This means participants cannot ask or signal for someone to pass them a piece. To end up with a completed square, *all other* members must take the initiative. They must see what pieces others require and reach over to give those pieces to them. In other words, the emphasis is on giving and cooperating.

Now imagine for a moment you are a student. How would you feel? In all probability, you'd feel happier and happier as the other group members noticed what pieces you needed and as you were able to reciprocate. In this way cooperative behavior is reinforced in emotional and practical terms. Teamwork is promoted by the realization that the success of each individual depends on the success of all. The emphasis is on giving and cooperating, and no reinforcement is given for being the fastest, smartest, or best in the group. On the contrary, success is achieved only through asking "How can we work together and help each other so we can all do the best job?"

At the end of the game, students in each group are given time to discuss how they completed the squares, what feelings they experienced, and what frustrations, if any, developed. This discussion itself is an important team-building activity. The students are looking not only at how they reacted as separate individuals, but also at their group process—how their group as a whole

THE BROKEN SQUARES GAME

Goals
- To analyze certain aspects of cooperation in solving a group problem.
- To sensitize participants to behaviors that may contribute toward or obstruct the solving of a group problem.

Group Size
- Any number of groups of six participants each. There will be five participants and an observer/judge. *Note:* If it is necessary to balance the size of the group, the observer/judge role may be eliminated from this activity.

Time Required
- Fifteen to 20 minutes for the exercise and an additional 15 minutes for discussion.

Materials
- Chalkboard, chalk, eraser.
- Tables that will seat five participants each, or students can sit on the floor.
- One set of broken squares for each group of five participants.

Physical Setting
- Tables should be spaced far enough apart so that the various groups cannot observe the activities of other groups.

Process

The teacher may wish to begin with a discussion of the meaning of co-operation; this should lead to suggestions by the groups of what is essential in successful group cooperation. These may be listed on the board, and the teacher may introduce the exercise by indicating that the groups will conduct an experiment to test their suggestions. Basic suggestions that the teacher may want to make to all group members are as follows:

- Understand the total problem.
- Understand how to contribute toward solving the problem,
- Be aware of the potential contributions of other individuals.
- Recognize the problems of other individuals in order to aid them in making their maximum contribution.

Instructions

When the preliminary discussion is finished, the teacher asks each group to distribute the envelopes from the prepared packets. The envelopes are to remain unopened until the signal to work is given. The teacher then reads the instructions to the group, calling for questions, or questioning groups as to their understanding of the instructions. It will be necessary for the teacher to monitor the tables during the exercise to enforce the rules established in the instructions.

When all the groups have completed the task, the teacher will engage the groups in a discussion of the experience. Discussion should focus on feelings rather than merely relating experiences and general observations. Observations are solicited from the observer/judge.

DIRECTIONS FOR MAKING A SET OF SQUARES

A set consists of five envelopes containing three pieces of cardboard that have been cut into different patterns and which, when properly arranged, will form five squares of equal size. One set should be provided for each group of five persons. For younger students, a picture pasted on one side before the squares are cut helps to simplify the task for them.

1. To prepare a set, cut out five cardboard squares of equal size, approximately six by six inches. Place the squares in a row and mark them as below, penciling the letters *a, b, c,* etc. lightly so that they can later be erased.
2. The lines should be so drawn that, when cut out, all pieces marked *a* (or *b* or *c* etc.) will be of exactly the same size. By using multiples of three inches, several combinations will enable participants to form one or two possible squares, but only one combination will form five six-by-six-inch squares.
3. After drawing the lines on the six-by-six-inch squares and labeling them with lowercase letters, cut each square as marked into smaller pieces to make the parts of the puzzle.
4. Mark five envelopes *v, w, x, y,* and *z.* Distribute the cardboard pieces in the envelopes as follows:

   Envelope *v* has pieces *i, h, e*
   Envelope *w* has pieces *a, a, a, c*
   Envelope *x* has pieces *a, j*
   Envelope *y* has pieces *d, f*
   Envelope *z* has pieces *g, b, f, c*

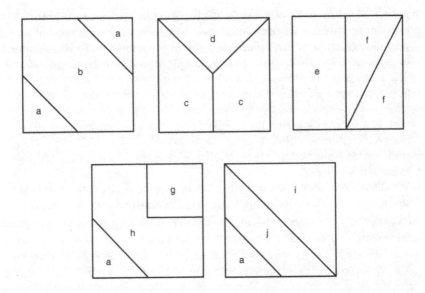

5. Erase the penciled letter from each piece and write, instead, the appropriate envelope letter. This will make it easy to return the pieces to the proper envelope for subsequent use when a group has completed the task.

RULES FOR BROKEN SQUARES GAME

Group Task

To complete five squares in such a way that each player has a square the same size as the other players. In other words, everybody must end up with the same size square.

Rules

This is a giving game, a group task. You will each get an envelope containing three pieces, but don't open it until you are told to. You will have 40 minutes to build your squares."[2] The game must be played in complete silence. No talking. You may not point or signal other players with your hands in any way. You may *not* place a piece in another player's square. You may not take a piece from another player. You *may* give a piece to another player. When you have finished, cover your square with your envelope.

[2] The NASA Game, an exercise in group problem solving that is more appropriate for older students, can be found in the Appendices.

worked. Learning to evaluate their group process is an important part of the jigsaw method because this is how students come to take responsibility' for their own behavior. We will discuss this in more detail later in the chapter, but first let us turn to another preliminary teambuilding activity, the development of listening skills.

Active Listening Many students may have developed a habit of not listening to their fellow classmates. Picture this situation: The teacher first calls on Christopher, who gives the wrong answer. He then calls on Julie, who is eagerly waving her hand. She gives the same wrong answer. How can this be? Doesn't she realize that answer is wrong? Actually, as most experienced teachers are well aware, this is not an uncommon occurrence. It happens because the student is watching her teacher for cues, signs of approval or disapproval that indicate whether the question is still available to be answered. In other words, Julie is simply not listening to Christopher. The importance of listening to a fellow student may never have occurred to her, not even as part of the strategy to win approval for herself, and certainly not as a means of learning something about the material under question. In a jigsaw classroom, however, if the students are not listening attentively to each other, they are not going to be able to learn what the other students are contributing. Moreover, listening to the others is the *only* way to learn the material.

Clearly it is advisable for the teacher to provide an opportunity for the students to work on developing listening skills before curriculum material is approached. Exercises such as the interview described under the section on team-building can be done in pairs, in groups, or as a class.

There is a further reason to impress upon students the importance of listening to each other. If the speaker in a group senses that she is not being listened to with interest or appreciation, she is likely to feel rejected and to lose the motivation and commitment to do well at teaching. For example, if Michele is intently drawing horses, Justin is folding paper airplanes, and two others are passing notes during Sara's presentation to her group, Sara is clearly without an audience. Of course she won't want to continue speaking. And the next time her turn comes up, Sara is not likely to be enthusiastic about preparing her material.

It is vital that steps be taken to prevent such a process of discouragement from getting started. That's the reason listening skills are an important part of team-building. In a more general sense, the preliminary teambuilding sessions can help students begin to learn what to do when a problem arises that makes the group experience less than satisfying. It is essential that the students eventually come to understand that whether the group process is satisfying or unsatisfying is really within their control. That is, each group member is somewhat responsible for the manner in which the group is functioning. Thus, if the groups were working on the question of making their group process more effective, each group of students might have five minutes to list 20 or 30 positive behaviors. The final list generated by this discussion could then be posted in the classroom for all to see. A point worth emphasizing is that it is more useful for these behaviors to be stated positively than negatively. As you no doubt know, a student learns more by thinking about what he ought to be doing, such as "listening while another member is talking," than he does by thinking about what he ought not to be doing, such as "not talking while someone else is speaking." The negative statement fails to lead him to positive behaviors that can be reinforced. It tells him only what not to do. Moreover, a discussion of this nature gives students practice with a positive language with which they can talk about their own group process.

The more specific these behavioral prescriptions, the better. For example, if students decide they should "show each other they are listening," the teacher might suggest they list the ways they are able to know that someone is listening to them. Behaviors such as this might be listed:

Look directly at the speaker.

Nod that you understand her.

Rephrase what she has just said.

Summarize her statements.

Reflect the feeling behind her statements. (If Jaime says, "My part was much harder to learn than the part you guys got," the listener might respond, "It sounds like you're feeling you got an unfair share of the work.")

Let the speaker know that you have heard by building on her ideas. (For example, "Besides what you've said, I think . . .")

Lean toward the speaker while listening.

Smile with reassurance.

In other words, look and behave as if you are really listening. All of these can later be practiced in role-playing activities. Once decided on, this list can be copied on posterboard or laminated and posted in the room as a reference.

What happens in such a brainstorming session is very significant: The students begin to think in terms of group process. But more important, it is the opening wedge in developing individual responsibility, when students begin to realize that they themselves are able to develop a cooperative learning environment. If a problem later arises in a jigsaw group, the students have specific standards by which to recognize it, diagnose it, and cope with it constructively. They will be able to try, effectively, to change the group process to make it more rewarding. The old familiar tactics of blaming someone, name-calling, whining, or simply withdrawing will be used much less frequently.

EVALUATING THE GROUP PROCESS

This skill of evaluating the group process is an important element of the jigsaw method. During team-building exercises, students often are asked to focus on certain questions: Are we sticking to the task? Are we encouraging everyone to participate? Are we listening to each other attentively? Are we treating each other with kindness and respect?

Once students begin an academic unit, group process evaluation is facilitated by using group-process cards, which each students fills out during the last five or ten minutes of the group session.

It is important that students actually write their impressions of the group rather than just think about them. Our experience shows that formally writing down an evaluation increases students' motivation to examine the group process and to commit themselves to improving it. We have also found that it is helpful to have each student write an individual opinion first and then to join the others in filling out a group card. In this way everyone has something specific in hand to share with the others. If students are not given the opportunity to write their opinions first, they will often merely say that everything is "okay" or "not bad," and let it go at that. The problem with this is twofold: (1) they are not exploring in depth the ways they might improve their group and (2) they are missing the chance to focus on the ways they are already doing a good job. In this last instance, they miss the rewards of seeing how well they are functioning and their positive behavior is not specifically reinforced.

Group Process Sheet

The group process sheet was designed as a form to help students become familiar with important aspects of the group process (see page 40). Some of the ideas from this sheet can be posted on a group process bulletin board in the classroom.

The following points should be remembered about the group process:

- It is important to let the person who is talking know that you are listening to what he or she is saying. Some ways you can do this are nodding, smiling, and asking questions.
- When you are involved in the jigsaw method, you do many different things each day, and you need to have time for each of them. Try to keep

track of how much time is left so you don't run out before you are done with everything.

- At the end of each day you will have a process discussion. You will answer several questions about what happened in your group that day and discuss them. These discussions are important because how well you will be able to learn the material depends on how well your group works together. Try to help see what problems your group is having, and come up with suggestions for solving them in these discussions.

The group process sheet is a list of questions that students can use to record what happens in their group each day. The first three questions can be discussed most days, and the other questions provide additional focus on specific issues. You may want to do one a day, or one at the beginning of a unit and again at the end. That way the development of the group functioning can be tracked through assigning a number to each answer and tabulating the results. This not only provides the teacher with information about the development of group process skills but also provides feedback to the groups to help them work together better.

INTERGROUP COMPETITION

So far in the chapter we have been emphasizing cooperation in the classroom. We now want to point out that there may still be a place for competition during the early transition phases, if that competition occurs *between* groups rather than *within* groups. Many teachers have found that when jigsaw groups are first established, group identity and group motivation are weak. In that case, a small amount of intergroup competition may stimulate children to become a "team." However, it can be effective but tricky business to try to use the well-practiced skills of competition to develop cooperative skills. The already established system has considerably more vigor through familiarity than the new one and can easily take over. It is important not to nurture intense feelings of competition between jigsaw groups. Because students from different jigsaw groups will have to work with each other in the "expert group" sessions, intergroup hostility will make this difficult.

Since many teachers use competition as part of their classroom management strategy, it is important to have students discuss the possible negative effects of such competition and the positive effects of intergroup cooperation. Eventually, this process will enable the various groups to begin cooperating. To facilitate this, the teacher might set up tasks in such a way that they can be more easily accomplished if the groups share their work. Or perhaps a bonus of some sort (extra points or extra privileges) can be given if all the groups do well.

A CHANGE IN MOTIVATION: LOOKING AHEAD

After two weeks of team-building activities, students will find they have some power to control their group process by solving the problems that inevitably arise as they learn to work together. Because of this, working together gradually becomes an increasingly pleasurable and productive experience. Now students are ready for a new task: using the jigsaw method to teach each other an academic subject.

GROUP PROCESS SHEET

1. What one word would you use to describe how your group was today? _____

2. What one word would describe the way you would like your group to be? _____

3. Is everyone participating?
   Yes, always_____ Usually_____ Occasionally_____ Rarely_____
   If not, why not?_____

4. In your group are you all trying to make each other feel good?
   Yes, always_____ Usually_____ Occasionally_____ Rarely_____
   If not, what are you doing?_____

5. Are you trying to help each other feel able to say what you think?
   Yes, always_____ Usually_____ Occasionally_____ Rarely_____

6. Are you listening to each other?
   Yes, always_____ Usually_____ Occasionally_____ Rarely_____

7. Are you *showing* that you are listening to each other?
   Yes, always_____ Usually_____ Occasionally_____ Rarely_____

8. Are you saying "That's good" to each other when you like something?
   Yes, always_____ Usually_____ Occasionally_____ Rarely_____

9. Are you asking each other questions?
   Yes, always_____ Usually_____ Occasionally_____ Rarely_____

10. Are you listening and really trying to answer these questions?
    Yes, always_____ Usually_____ Occasionally_____ Rarely_____

11. Are you paying attention to each other?
    Yes, always_____ Usually_____ Occasionally_____ Rarely_____

12. Is any one person talking most of the time?
    Yes, always_____ Usually_____ Occasionally_____ Rarely_____

An interesting change soon becomes apparent in what motivates students to learn academic material. Previously, student drive was based on the desire to *be* best in relation to other students, not to *do* one's best. In competitive classes students might work very hard but not necessarily for the joy of learning as much as they can. Instead, the motivation more often is the pleasure of attaining a comparative advantage over the other students in academic grades, in the esteem of the teacher, and so forth. Although anxiety-provoking, this competitive environment can be motivating for the successful students. Unfortunately for the slower students who are not "winners," who cannot beat the others in academic performance, it all too often leads to discouragement and lowered motivation.

However, as students carry what they have learned from team-building sessions into jigsaw groups, the motivation to outperform others becomes tempered and is replaced by a sense of responsibility[7] to the group, by the desire to help others and to share ideas. Importantly, this desire does not dampen performance—it improves it. Children find that the joy of discovery can be enhanced when shared with others. When learning occurs in a low-anxiety atmosphere of mutual acceptance, it becomes more rewarding; it is, simply, more fun. Teachers often find additional changes occurring in their classrooms. One of our teachers, during the third week of using jigsaw, wrote this:

> It is exciting to see that Michele and Teri, two outstanding students, now seem to be more challenged by helping the slow students than by trying to impress me and the other students with how smart they are. In fact, their cooperativeness has transferred to non-jigsaw modes of learning. For example, recently Michele sensed that Bill was having trouble with his division problems. Without hesitation, she quietly pulled up a chair and began to help him. Bill was able to accept her help appreciatively. As other students in the class began to notice how well Bill was doing in math, they came over to Michele for help. Now Michele gives help to anyone who needs it, and so does Teri.

Again, it would be naive to expect this kind of behavior to occur early in the process. Indeed, in the beginning of jigsaw learning, some students might express frustration at the change of atmosphere. It is vital for the teacher to help these students adapt to their new role as "teacher-learner" rather than as competitor.

CHAPTER 4

JIGSAW: THE PIECES OF THE PUZZLE

Before we take a look at the jigsaw method as a whole, let's examine the various pieces that go into making up the jigsaw classroom.

STUDENTS

We have found that young children—even kindergartners—are perfectly able and willing to engage in cooperative behavior. At the same time, we should note that our attempts to institute the jigsaw technique prior to the fourth grade have not always gone smoothly. There are two major issues. First, virtually all of the students in a group need at least a minimal proficiency in reading for jigsaw to work; one cannot always count on this general proficiency among all children in the first few grades. Second, the understanding of the basic elements of jigsawing requires a certain degree of conceptual ability. While we have found that most six-year-olds can eventually grasp what is required, it often necessitates a longer period of time to thoroughly acquaint them with the system than is the case for youngsters ten years old and above.

At the upper end of the classroom continuum, there seems to be no limit. Middle school and high school level groups work particularly well. At the university level, students can be placed in jigsaw groups and meet on their own time outside of class. Each student is responsible for a portion of the reading material (a number of research articles, one aspect of a subject area, and so forth). Students then report to their group and discuss the topics. The only intervention made by the instructor consists of a brief training session designed to spell out the degree of specificity required in the actual reporting. This is so that a semblance of uniformity can be achieved. That is, in technical reporting it is conceivable that if the students are not instructed, some reports might be overly detailed and others might be too sparse. A brief instruction about the appropriate degree of complexity can be invaluable. Virtually all of the university students who have used the jigsaw reported good results: they mastered the material in far less time than if they had read it on their own, plus they had the added enjoyment of companionship and the intellectual stimulation brought about by the sharing of a variety of perspectives.

Another way jigsaw has been used is during teacher training workshops that require covering reading material in a short period of time. In this case, participants are assigned individual chapters and given time to read. Next, expert groups are formed, comprised of those assigned the first section of the material, those assigned the second part, and so forth. After discussing the key points of what they have just read, they plan the best ways to communicate this information to others. After this, groups are reformed so that all the reading material is covered within a single group and group members share their knowledge with each other. This method has been used as a quick and efficient way of covering as much as an entire volume in a one-day workshop.

CURRICULUM

A carefully planned curriculum can go a long way toward making students' introduction to jigsaw go smoothly. Ideally, the teacher will have prepared the curriculum during a school vacation or other nonteaching time, giving the task uninterrupted attention and making the process of designing the curriculum a pleasant one. If this is not feasible, we strongly recommend that the preparation of the curriculum be completed—at least—before jigsawing actually begins.

A wide variety of subject matter can be adapted for use with the jigsaw format. On the whole, narrative material that emphasizes reading and comprehension skills is the easiest to work with in groups. Because of this, the area of social studies—including history, civics, geography and so forth—is perhaps the most naturally suited to the technique. The major skills involved are reading and comprehension. Jigsaw has been successfully used, however, in teaching math, language arts, and biology, although those subjects are more difficult to adapt.

We have also found that jigsaw works best with material that is *not* conceptually novel (requiring students to use skills they have not yet learned). Just as we would not attempt to assign *The Life of Joseph Pulitzer* to a group of children who have not learned to read, by the same token we would not assign "subtraction" to a group of students who have not yet acquired this skill. Thus introducing addition or subtraction for the first time in the context of a jigsaw group is probably not a good idea, although jigsaw could certainly be used for practicing these skills. We know of teachers who have successfully employed the jigsaw method for the instruction of math, language arts, science, English as a second language, and other subjects that required new skills to be learned. In these areas jigsaw has been used primarily to review material previously taught by more traditional methods.

The jigsaw method presents another limitation with reading assignments that are cumulatively interwoven and must be read in sequence. For example, while it would be easy to grasp Joseph Pulitzer's middle years without knowing about his childhood and young adulthood, it would be far more difficult to make sense out of Chapter 3 of a detective story without having first read Chapters 1 and 2. Accordingly, if you are a fifth-grader assigned to part three of a story or subject matter that is, by its very nature, cumulatively interwoven, chances are you will not be able to grasp its meaning sufficiently well to communicate it meaningfully to members of your jigsaw group. *This is the key to adapting curriculum for jigsaw: Whatever material is used must be divided into coherent segments that can be distributed to members of the jigsaw group.* That is, an individual piece of the lesson must be understandable to a student without knowledge of the other portions given to his groupmates.

It is advisable for teachers to include in their weekly lesson planning the material to be covered daily in the jigsaw group and to provide additional time for curriculum preparation. Homework assignments and material to supplement the basic lesson should also be organized well in advance.

Jigsaw Cards

Almost any sturdy material can be used for the construction of jigsaw cards, with four-by-six-inch index cards being the first choice. If the information is from a textbook or other resource, paragraphs can be copied and glued onto the index cards with rubber cement. Illustrations, diagrams, or other relevant material can be glued to the back of the card.

Rather than let students pick their own cards (sometimes they will pick the one that is the most eye-catching or has the least amount of writing), you might want to pencil each student's name at the top of a card. This will help balance the groups (including the expert groups) since you will know ahead of time who will have each part.

To provide for maximum interdependence among group members, each student should have access to other parts of the lesson only through other group members. Clearly, those students who have already had experience with the lesson material will be less dependent on listening to their groupmates to learn that material.[1]

The amount of material used and how it is broken up are both important aspects of curriculum preparation for jigsaw. In the first few weeks, students

---

[1] As mentioned in Chapter 2, Robert Slavin has devised an alternative method called Jigsaw II. As with the original jigsaw, group members in Jigsaw II also become experts on one part of the material, meet in expert groups, and are responsible for their group members learning that portion of the material. However, in Jigsaw II, all students in the group read the entire assignment rather than having to depend solely on group members for the information. Group members then take individual tests on the material, the results of which contribute to a team score.

A1. Our country is made up of many different groups of people. They have all helped to make America the nation that it is today. The groups we will be looking at are the Native Americans, Europeans, Asians, Africans, and South Americans. These groups of people were all given different names because of the continents which they originally came from. For example, the Europeans originally came from Europe, the Africans from Africa, and so on. The people who lived within each of these continents were also given other names according to which country or area they lived in. For example, the Chinese and the Japanese people are both considered Asians because China and Japan are both in Asia. People were also given other names for many different reasons. For example, the Native Americans were called "Indians" because when Christopher Columbus first discovered America he thought that what he had really found was a place called the "West Indies." Another example is that the African people were given the names "Negroes" and "Blacks" because of their dark skin color.

A3. Some cultures are made up of many smaller cultures put together. For example the "European Culture" is made up of the separate cultures of each of the countries which are in Europe. Even within each country there might be several different cultures. For example, in the United States people from many different cultures live and work together, but at the same time each of these people might practice their own cultural traditions. What other places can you think of where there are many smaller cultures which make up one large culture? How much material constitutes a full load when using jigsaw? In our experience students can be given as much material as is used in traditional teaching methods—or even more. The students seem to rise to the occasion.

are still adjusting to the process as well as learning content material. We suggest that at least initially the amount of information be kept quite light. After two weeks, the workload can be gradually increased until a full load is reached. We have found that time lost early in the process is made up later—with interest.

The decision about how much material should be contained on each card is a particularly important one. If there is consistently too little material, there will be little challenge for the students, and they wall quickly become bored with the process. On the other hand, if there is too much material, it will be difficult to cover all parts within the allotted time; this is bound to be a frustrating experience for the group. One way to avoid these extremes is to equate the number of important facts that each jigsaw card contains. Thus one student may read three paragraphs and another five, but they will both be responsible for the same number of important facts. Using this method results in a student's workload varying from day to day, but we have not found this to impede the successful working of the group.

An additional policy we have found helpful is breaking up material so that a separate subject is covered each day of jigsawing (Monday—geography of China; Tuesday—Chinese family structure; and so forth). The best general advice we can give concerning the division of material is to strive for a balanced distribution among individual students and over the course of the unit.

EXPERT GROUPS

If a class is to use jigsaw an hour a day, 20 minutes of the hour should be spent in expert groups and the remaining 40 minutes in the jigsaw group. At the beginning of the hour, students gather in their jigsaw groups to receive their paragraphs and any special instructions from their group leader. They then break into expert groups (consisting of those students with identical paragraphs) to plan their presentation.

Once in the expert group the students first read their cards. It is helpful to the poor readers if one person reads the card aloud. Then group members start helping each other understand the material on the card. They work on meanings of words, think up examples to explain things, and so forth. Students can ask questions about anything that is unclear. Students who grasp the material quickly are a vital resource in helping slower students learn the material. When everybody understands the information on the card, the group decides how to teach the material to the jigsaw groups. Expert group members thus get an idea of how the others are planning to present their material, hear some suggestions that may aid their own presentation, and give each other constructive feedback.

Expert groups have additional advantages. Even the brightest student is stimulated by the questions, examples, and trial presentations of the experts. The expert group may also be considered an effective device to remedy list-lessness on one of those dull, low-energy days that descend from time to time on every classroom. A typical jigsaw group stays intact for a period of six to ten weeks, long enough so that the children in it may occasionally get bored with each other and may want the excitement of a temporary change in rou-tine. On the other hand, they may decidedly not want such a change because they have become so comfortable with their teammates; they know exactly what to expect of each other and patterns of interaction have become estab-lished and easy. In either case, the expert group challenges them to make new interpersonal adaptations without disrupting the smoothly functioning jigsaw learning group. Finally, as jigsaw group identity solidifies, the groups may be tempted to view each other competitively. Temporary restructuring with ex-pert groups builds bonds across groups, thus helping to keep such intergroup competition from becoming pervasive.

Expert groups present several special problems, however, because they are not ongoing working units like the jigsaw groups; they change with the cur-riculum. Since the same people do not meet regularly, they have no chance to develop the cohesiveness that results from the team-building exercises. Ini-tially students may have more trouble working with each other in expert groups, but as the jigsaw groups become used to working together and develop cohesion, the expert groups improve as well. As mentioned before, it is im-portant to avoid intense feelings of competition between jigsaw groups since students from one jigsaw group will have to work with students from other jigsaw groups in the expert sessions.

There is another problem with expert groups. The students may not imme-diately be comfortable working with each other, particularly when the jigsaw process is new to them. They may even have difficulty getting organized and down to work. Teachers generally find it advisable to pick a responsible and capable leader even for these temporary groups. It is also helpful, on occasion, to run through a quick team-building exercise to establish a cooperative mood. Once the jigsaw process becomes familiar, cooperative attitudes tend to carry over from group to group.

Expert Group Leadership

It is impossible for expert groups to have regular leaders since the group com-position changes daily. Leaving the groups leaderless creates problems, how-ever. A leaderless expert group has trouble getting organized and accomplishing the day's business. We have tried having expert groups pick their own leaders; this seems to work well with two qualifications: (1) those students who are seen as natural leaders are the ones who are always chosen, and (2) when there is no natural leader among the members of the group, it seems hard for the group to get organized enough to pick any leader at all.

As an alternative, we suggest that the teacher select expert leaders before the day's session and announce them to the class. This alleviates the necessity for the group to pick its own leader and saves time in organization.

It is a good idea for students to have notebooks with them in expert groups and to take very short "key word" notes. However, we strongly discourage letting students write out what they are going to say and then read it. Short notes give them about the right amount of help with their parts, and of course learning to take good notes is a valuable skill for students to have.

JIGSAW GROUPS

Having finished working in their expert groups, the students reassemble in their jigsaw groups. The teacher labels jigsaw curriculum cards in a specific order, and the students should teach them in this order. After the jigsaw groups get back together, the student who has card number one begins presenting. If the group is restless and having trouble settling down, the group leader should make an intervention—saying, for example, "I'd like to get started now," or "I'm having trouble hearing Mike because you're talking." The student who is trying to make a presentation might also say something—for example, "It makes me feel bad when you don't listen to me."

The students in the group should be encouraged to use active listening skills. A student who is drawing pictures or looking down is showing no overt interest in the procedure. A short time (five or ten minutes) should be reserved at the end of the hour for the group to discuss any problems that have arisen in the hour.

After the individual presentations, the group can review all parts together. Each student may try to think of three important points from the lesson. Or students may ask each other questions about the lesson and try to answer questions on parts other than their own. Having such a review ensures that every student understands the lesson. If a review is not done, students may leave with an incorrect understanding of the information.

Finally, students in the jigsaw group should fill out the group process sheet and take five or ten minutes to discuss the day's process sheet. Process discussions are feedback sessions and allow the students to express their feelings, talk about problems they feel the group is having, and attempt to find solutions to these problems.

OTHER PIECES: SPECIAL ROLES

The Teacher's Role as Facilitator

To understand techniques that student leaders will be learning and practicing, let us begin by observing Mr. Cross, a jigsaw teacher (the students' leader's model) at work. He is moving about the classroom from group to group, checking how each group is progressing on its task, keeping eyes and ears open for any problems that may be developing. One of the students calls out to him in exasperation, "Mr. Cross, Nicholas won't listen." It is *not* the responsibility of Mr. Cross to solve the problem with an order such as "Nicholas, get to work immediately," although this might be the case in a more traditional setting. Instead, he might ask the group leader what the students themselves have done to solve the problem. For example, he might ask if the group is doing everything it can to help Nicholas understand the material. In this way, he is reminding the students of their responsibility to help one another learn. The leader might then ask Nicholas if he is listening and, if not, what's the source of the problem. Nicholas may not be listening because the study topic—the parts of a plant—is being presented too rapidly for him to follow. In such a case, the teacher might suggest to the leader that she ask one of the quicker students to review the facts for everyone.

Another possibility may be that Nicholas is merely bored by the way the material is being presented. Perhaps Scott is simply reading it off a card in a halting monotone. The teacher sees that Scott has not really mastered his material, so he may call the leader aside and suggest that she try to get Scott to put the material into his own words or relate it to something in his own life that the others could understand and relate to as well. In this case, Mr. Cross would be helping all the children understand how to approach and penetrate any new material.

Finally, there may be times when the teacher judges it necessary to set aside the academic material altogether. A quick review of something the students discussed during earlier team-building sessions may be in order. For example, he might respond to the complaint about Nicholas by asking the students to focus on group process: "What steps might be taken here to encourage full participation?" The group, when given the opportunity, can usually come up with a creative and effective solution for its own problems, a solution that is often better than the one the teacher suggests.

It is important to emphasize here that, from the beginning, teachers should make interventions through the student group leader whenever possible. This will establish and validate the leader's facilitating role for the other students. Bypassing the leader will undermine that student's commitment to help, which in the long run means the students will continue their dependence on the

45

teacher as chief problem solver. Thus it is best to phrase requests for interventions as suggestions to the leader: "Perhaps you should check to see if everybody understands those facts now" or "You might tell the group that calling Nicholas names is not going to help them learn the material." The questions and words chosen will be picked up by the group leaders in a modeling process that speeds the development of effective groups under student guidance.

In addition to acting as a consultant-facilitator for the various groups, the teacher is also an information resource, making available interesting academic materials. Thus when a student asks a question on a particular subject the teacher can answer with another question: "Where could you look that up?" Or the teacher can refer the questioner to other students. One teacher we know has a classroom rule that states simply: "Three before me." She will answer questions only after a student has asked three other students for help. Again, the intent is to guide students toward greater independence—and, to guide them toward interdependence: "Lisa, could you show Luis how to use that reference book you were using yesterday?"

Giving up authority is understandably difficult for some teachers. However, for most it is exciting to watch the responsibility for learning shift to the students. Rather than pouring information into students' heads, the teacher's role becomes that of a learning gardener, cultivating the proper atmosphere and setting for learning. Eventually, this learning becomes a matter of student responsibility, which means that no longer can they blame the teacher for a boring class or a dull discussion. If the classroom environment is not a rewarding one for students, they know they can and should do something about it. The power and skill are theirs.

Even so, it is obvious that teachers cannot abdicate all authority; they cannot simply turn the student loose in a hit-or-miss fashion. Behind the scenes they must design a structure, a step-by-step procedure to help students learn how to make use of each other effectively. In each classroom there should always be firm boundaries within which the groups function. The alert teacher carefully notes the pace at which the students can successfully take charge and then works within those boundaries. Let's look more closely at how to facilitate the development of effective group leaders.

The Student Group Leader

During team-building sessions, you may wish to stress the usefulness of a group leader. You can do so by having children focus on the specific ways a leader should function in order to be effective. The same technique that group members used to brainstorm a list of their own tasks and responsibilities can be employed with respect to the group leader. Here are some examples of the tasks and responsibilities of the group leader that was generated by a group of students:

- Helps get the group organized.
    Gets folder.[2]
    Appoints a timekeeper and recorder to take notes on the day's events.
    Convenes and adjourns the group.
    Helps the group discuss the process of how they interact.
    Helps set the agenda.
- Keeps the group on task by reminding them of the work at hand by asking the recorder to read what has been discussed, by asking the timekeeper how much time is remaining, and so forth.
- Serves as a liaison between the teacher and the group.
    Understands and/or clarifies assignments with the teacher before trying to describe them to the group.
- Shows enthusiasm for task and does not say, "This is what we have to do today because the teacher said so."
- Models productive member behavior.
- Asks questions for information and/or clarification, never just to show off.
- Is patient and understanding; believes that the team can be effective if it follows certain rules of working together.
- Politely asks members to do things.
- Helps the group deal with disagreements by staying impartial and helping members to understand each other rather than finding blame. (For example, asks members: "What's bothering you?" "Can you be more specific?" "How can you help things go better?" Is this what you mean?")
- Encourages feedback about how to be more helpful: "How can I do it better next time?"

Although each group generates its own list, the lists are usually remarkably similar. Composing this list permits the students in each group to have some influence on how its future leader will act. In a sense, the group is giving its leader permission to follow the list. However, it should be clear that having a leader does not relieve the members of their own responsibilities. For this reason many teachers post the list for member behavior beside that for leader behavior, for ready reference once the jigsaw groups begin.

---

[2] The folder generally contains the group-process cards and a summary of the work done to date.

Selecting Leaders

Since teachers need help they can count on when first establishing the jigsaw process, they usually select the group leaders themselves, choosing reliable students who can handle extra responsibility. Such students may in fact thrive on the extra challenge; it can function to keep their interest in school alive. Later on, however, leadership can rotate among the members of each group. We would like to emphasize that over the course of a school year, each student should have the opportunity to be trained as a group leader. Once the model for group leadership has been established and demonstrated, subsequent training should go quickly and smoothly.

Group leaders do require some special training. At first the teacher may simply meet with them informally, perhaps over lunch, to explain the jigsaw process and to discuss their role. Then as the jigsaw experience gets underway, such meetings can be held once or twice a week to give the leaders continuing support and an opportunity to share problems and solutions. We will suggest here, however, a training process somewhat more structured than a casual lunch-hour discussion. Our observation, supported by teacher experience, indicates that this training is well worth setting aside special time for. This is particularly true in the beginning, when all the students are unfamiliar with jigsaw group experience.

TRAINING GROUP LEADERS

There are essentially two parts to this training process for the group leaders: (1) discussions on some aspect of how to lead a jigsaw group and (2) role-playing of difficult group situations. For example, in the first lesson for student leaders, the teacher conducts a ten-minute discussion on leader behavior. At the end of this discussion, she asks students to review her leadership behavior: Which of her behaviors helped the group? Which ones hindered it? Since this is the first lesson, and since she is the teacher, her request might meet with total silence. In this case she would have to probe with more questions: "Do you remember when Josh and Tracy were talking at the same time? Do you remember what I said, how we solved that problem?" She might continue with this observation: "I think perhaps I wasn't fair to Jim. I wanted to finish quickly and so I interrupted him too soon. How else could I have acted without hurting someone's feelings and yet still gotten the group to finish its work?"

By exposing herself to criticism, the teacher, a traditional authority figure, is setting an important example. A leader, whether teacher or student, is still part of the group. He or she can always benefit from having constructive behavior praised and mistakes pointed out tactfully. The goal is to have an effective group in which each student can learn, and it is essential for the leader to help the group reach that goal. Training sessions, then, include a discussion of some issue, followed by a critique of the quality of leadership displayed during the discussion.

The second aspect of leadership training involves role-playing. The teacher asks group leaders to brainstorm problem situations they might encounter.

Role-Playing Problem Situations

Here are some examples of the type of problem situations that group leaders might come up with when brainstorming:

- Some members never talk.
- One member dominates the discussion.
- Members call each other names.
- Certain members will not work.
- One member wants to work alone.
- Everyone talks at once.

Next group leaders choose the three most commonly raised issues and talk briefly about ways to handle them. The group then role-plays each of the three situations. After each role-play, the student who played the leader receives feedback from others on what he did that was effective in dealing with the problem and what other things he might have tried. During this critique, the teacher encourages students to discuss the costs and benefits of each possible leader behavior. At this point, it is helpful to role-play the same situation again and compare the results with the first attempt. Then the group can summarize the general leadership behaviors that are effective in each situation. Let us summarize this process:

1. The students list problem situations with which they will be concerned.
2. They role-play the situations.
3. They critique what has just occurred.
4. They role-play again.
5. They develop general principles for intervening.

We have found this to be an extremely effective training procedure. The rationale for each of these steps follows.

Listing Problem Situations   Step 1 increases students' motivation to learn ways to deal with problem situations. Any technique that involves students in setting their own goals for what should be learned raises their commitment to reach those goals.

Role-Playing Situations   Step 2 accomplishes two things: Most importantly it permits students to experience beforehand various situations in an enjoyable way. They have a chance to practice new leadership behaviors and to become accustomed to leading difficult groups. Of almost equal importance, role-playing develops empathy; that is, students experience what it feels like to be the type of student whose role they are playing. For example, if one student plays a shy, withdrawn group member who is being pushed to participate, he may actually begin to experience the fear and resentment that a shy student might feel when being pressured. Learning this can aid group leaders in being more sensitive to a variety of students and hence, more helpful.

Critiquing the Role-Play   Step 3 is an exciting way to encourage students to develop their skills for analyzing group dynamics. Because they have just experienced the situation, each member is an expert on how another member's behavior affected his own feelings and responses. When students share the way they feel about each other during the role-playing, they increase their awareness of how different behaviors cause various reactions. For example, Susan might say, "When you ordered me to be quiet, I got mad because you were so bossy and I wanted to quit this group." Because they were just "playing a role" and were not really very emotionally involved, they can discuss what happened more openly and without too much need to explain or defend what they did. This also helps them become more comfortable giving and receiving feedback, an important skill for a group leader to develop.

Second Role-Play   Step 4 helps students to learn and practice the modifications suggested by the group.

Intervention   Step 5, developing the general principles for intervening as a leader flows directly from the critiquing done in Step 3. As students talk about how they felt and acted when the leader said one thing and how they might have behaved if he had said another, they begin to see that each behavior has certain potential benefits and potential costs. **For** example, they might role-play what to do if two students are joking and laughing rather than working. The leader might intervene by saying. "We need to complete this task, and you two need to help. Sit up and pay attention." When critiquing, it would become clear that firm direction like this might work with, and even be needed by, some students but might only create resistance and resentment among others.

In addition even if it were effective in getting members to work (a benefit) it might cause them to become dependent on the group (a cost). A less directive approach—for example, "How can we encourage each person to do his work?"—might get the group to solve the problem itself (a benefit), but might take 15 minutes and result in some frustration over the failure to get further in the assigned task (a cost).

From discussions like these, the leaders will develop an awareness that there are few ways to behave in a group that are totally "right" or totally "wrong," but that some ways may be more appropriate than others in certain situations. After weighing the costs and benefits in different situations, they will slowly develop their own general principles to guide their decisions. For example, they will learn that the more authoritarian and directive they are, the faster work will get accomplished at the beginning. However, at some point giving orders will foster dependency and apathy, followed by resentment and resistance. Discussing these group issues gives the students an increasing awareness of how to be effective discussion leaders.

This then is the leadership-training procedure most teachers who are experienced in the jigsaw method would recommend. It takes time—perhaps two or three 30to 40-minute sessions a week for the first couple of weeks, and thereafter once every three weeks or so until the leaders change. When new group leaders are selected later in the year, they will need far less training because they will have participated in jigsaw groups and learned from the leaders of their groups.

MANAGING THE CLASS WHILE TRAINING LEADERS

A key question remains: What are all the other children doing while the teacher is involved with the leaders? If there is a teacher aide available, or another teacher who is also setting up a jigsaw classroom, the two can share responsibilities. During the preliminary team-building days, the other teacher or aide could be overseeing team-building exercises with the rest of the class. Thereafter, while the leaders are training, other students could perhaps be at work developing curriculum materials. For example, they could be drawing or cutting out pictures to supplement the lessons they will attempt to teach their teammates. The daily life of a typical classroom, as any teacher knows, necessitates intricate scheduling. The time and energy devoted to leader training, however, will be worth it, even if it means slightly more planning and more work, because the result will be effective leaders helping their groups work productively and with enjoyment. The positive behaviors that result will generalize to other situations both in and out of the classroom.

The training of leaders is not simply the learning of a limited practical skill by a select group of students. Indeed, the entire endeavor can be regarded as a unit teaching the behavior of small groups. Such experiential learning can be invaluable in helping students to gain insight into effective and ineffective processes in any problem-solving group, from congressional committees and city council meetings to their own families planning a vacation. Moreover, since leadership in jigsaw groups rotates, virtually all of the students will have the opportunity to benefit from this unique learning situation.

HOW JIGSAW WORKS

If the class is of average size, it probably will be divided into four to six jigsaw groups. Clearly, even with a teacher's aide, the teacher cannot be everywhere at once. The group leaders function as additional assistants to the teacher, channeling group process skills to group members and helping organize the activities of the day.

A goal in the jigsaw method is to have students regard each other, not only the teacher, as learning resources. *The teacher does not abandon all authority in the classroom, however.* Instead he acts as a backstage designer, creating a structure where the students may learn how best to make use of each other's knowledge and skills. The teacher moves around the room, from jigsaw group to jigsaw group, listening, observing, and keeping alert for any problems that may develop. Whenever possible, he makes interventions in group process through the group leader, thereby validating the group leader's authority for the other students. Since getting the group to regulate itself rather than to depend on the teacher is the object, interventions should help the group discover its own solutions. The teacher may phrase interventions as requests or suggestions to the group leader. (For example, "Jane, perhaps you should check to see if everyone feels they understand all the parts well enough to take a test tomorrow." Or, "Peter, maybe you should ask the group if telling John that he's stupid is helping them learn the material.")

If a group member complains directly to the teacher about someone in the group ("Mr. West, Jane is drawing funny pictures instead of listening!"), it is not the responsibility" of the teacher to solve the problem directly. The jigsaw teacher refers the problem back to the group to have them solve the problem themselves. In the example given above, Mr. West might ask the group leader whether group members have any idea why Jane is drawing pictures instead of listening. Perhaps the presentations are going too fast for her to understand, or perhaps she is bored because the speaker is reading his card in a dull tone of voice. Once the source of the problem has been identified, the teacher may take the group leader aside and suggest ways of solving it, or the students may be ready to take responsibility for finding their own solutions.

Teacher interventions have a clear function: to help students learn content more effectively and to help them develop an efficient, comfortable, and co-operative process. Perhaps most important, the teacher models for the students an effective jigsaw process. Through his interventions, even phrasing, tone of voice, and the kinds of suggestions he makes, the teacher provides an example students can eventually imitate in their roles as group members. The teacher can usefully make several types of interventions at different stages of the jigsaw process.

The first time expert groups meet, students may have difficulty finding effective, interesting ways of presenting their material. The teacher can help them learn how to extract important points from the printed information and think of creative ways to present what they have learned. The first time students present, they often simply read their paragraphs aloud—a boring experience for the listeners. The teacher might intervene in such a situation with the following suggestions:

- Can you think of a way to put the information you just learned into your own words?
- Can you think of how the material you just read is related to your own life? Are there any examples in your own life you could use in explaining this to your groupmates?
- Do you know what you are going to say when you go back to your jigsaw group?

Once students return to the jigsaw groups, they may need encouragement in their actual presentations. At the beginning some may have difficulty summarizing material in their own words. Even after experience in the expert group, they may simply read the paragraph aloud in the jigsaw group. You will need to remind them gently that putting the information in their own words makes their presentations more interesting and easier to follow. You should also encourage them to include the examples and interesting points discussed in the expert group and to comment on the presentation of other members.

Initially—in both expert and jigsaw groups—students may stop working together and become merely six individuals working alone who happen to be sharing a space. This may happen because they are practicing their own parts while others are talking. The teacher must emphasize that the purpose of the expert groups is for students with the same material to help each other and to learn from each other. The following interventions are useful in reminding students of this:

- Are you helping one another learn the material?
- Is everybody in this group understanding the material you covered today?

Sometimes quick students finish learning the material early and withdraw from the rest of the discussion, leaving other group members to struggle by themselves. This is the time for the teacher to emphasize the students role as teacher as well as student. Bright students need not disappear when they have learned the material. Rather they should be encouraged to spend the extra time helping other students learn. We have found that taking this role in the group can be rewarding for bright students and helps prevent them from getting bored. Having students fulfill this function may also narrow the social and communication gap between high achievers and low achievers that is often found in traditional classrooms. Teachers can use an intervention such as the following to encourage more able students to help their groupmates:

- Now that you've learned the material, can you help John learn it so he can teach it to his groupmates?

Perhaps the most important intervention the teacher will make is convincing students that fighting, teasing, and insulting each other are dysfunctional behaviors. Working in groups invariably involves some conflict. The teacher will find that some of the quicker students become impatient with those who learn more slowly; that some older students have misgivings about cooperating with others; and that existing rivalries tend to get exaggerated in the group setting. However, once the skills have been developed, jigsaw can be an excellent place to work out some of these conflicts and build understanding and harmonious relations.

CHAPTER 5

EXAMINING THE PIECES OF THE PUZZLE: SOLVING PROBLEMS IN THE JIGSAW CLASSROOM

While research continues to demonstrate numerous advantages of cooperative learning, this does not mean that the method is problem free. Certain problems do occur—but teachers have devised a variety of solutions for dealing with them. This chapter focuses on some of the more common problems, together with suggestions for how they might be handled. Many of these problems are not unique to the jigsaw method and neither are the solutions. But, as we saw earlier, the jigsaw method often illuminates problems that are hidden in more competitive classroom dynamics. More importantly, though, the jigsaw method often provides solutions that otherwise would be less readily available.

PROBLEM: THE NEED FOR COMMUNICATION SKILLS

Teasing, feuding, putting each other down—these activities, unfortunately, are as much a part of life in the classroom as reading and math. They take place in virtually all classrooms, in all sections of the country, at all grade levels and in all classroom structures. In the jigsaw classroom, children work in small groups, in very close association with each other. Because of this, conflict may seem more frequent, particularly at first, than in a competitive classroom. The great advantage of jigsaw is that this structure allows children to develop conflict resolution skills—so that they can solve their own problems as they occur. This is particularly true if these skills are emphasized as part of the school culture. Fortunately, in many school systems today children enter the middle elementary school grades with at least a modicum of experience at conflict resolution on the playground. The importance and usefulness of having a process to solve problems is therefore not brand new to them and in many cases they have already practiced many of the necessary skills. For example, many youngsters have learned not to interrupt others, and that name calling and put-downs are not effective.

The children in a jigsaw classroom are not individually isolated units. They are not forced by the arrangement of the classroom to curtail their conflicts and postpone them until recess. Moreover, any group (such as the one described in the previous chapter) has certain built-in conflicts attributable to the age of the children. Among third- and fourth-grade girls, best friend/best enemy conflicts sometimes interfere with classroom peace; among eleven- and twelve-year-olds, feelings of attraction and annoyance may run strong especially between children of different sexes. A boy and girl may regard each other with familiar suspicion, but a degree of interest may also begin to emerge. One day they may show exaggerated horror at finding they must sit together, the next they may seem to enjoy working together, or vice versa.

Besides these complexities, there are the conflicts that arise around academic tasks. A certain amount of material must be covered by tomorrow, but someone is holding back the group. Someone else is pushing ahead too rapidly and leaving the others behind in confusion. Because the jigsaw group tends to bring conflicts to the surface, it provides the setting and the tools for the children to work through those conflicts and learn something about themselves and one another in the process. Moreover, because only a few children are involved, the rest of the class need not be interrupted in its work. Accordingly, the teacher may decide to use an instance of petty quarreling as a vehicle to help the children learn about how their behavior affects others.

To demonstrate how to do this, we will use an obvious instance of negative communication. Name-calling is a pervasive American cultural tradition. Nicknames are sometimes seen as signs of affection, but in reality, they are often used to express negative feelings about someone. We call members of our family "honey" or "sweetie" but sometimes there is cruelty attached to the names we call others. Let's look at an example. Jason is a boy who like most children watches television an average of five hours a day. In almost every show, whether a police show, cartoon, or comedy, somebody gets called a name by someone else. It may be for laughs, but Jason comes to know that name-calling is a common way of interacting with others, one that gets a reaction out of others. Life seems to mirror television: When Jason's older sister stays out too late with her boyfriend, dad might get angry and in his anger, refers to her boyfriend as a slacker. And when Jason's mother opens the latest car repair bill, she might mutter something to the effect that the mechanic who failed to fix her car properly is an idiot and a thief. It is understandable that Jason comes to believe that name-calling is what you do to express displeasure. Even children with well-developed conflict resolution skills that include the dictum "no put-downs," sometimes fail to recognize the sting of name-calling.

With such experience behind him, Jason goes to school and settles down in his jigsaw group to complete some work for a test tomorrow. But alas Sara, one of Jason's groupmates, has her Civil War battles all mixed up. "You idiot,"

Jason says somewhat mildly. "I am not, you creep," Sara replies heatedly. The task is forgotten; the squabble is on.

What is going on here? What kind of intervention is needed? It may help to look at this brief interaction as a chain of events. Jason has some feelings and, at least in part, he expresses them. Sara perceives that his verbal behavior is directed against her, and it arouses certain feelings in her, feelings that Jason may have had no intention of arousing. It is natural for Sara, in her hurt and anger, to interpret Jason's intentions wrongly. She evaluates Jason as a person by calling him a name just as he called her a name.

Now let's fill in the particulars. By calling Sara an idiot, Jason has revealed his impatience but not his anxiety about the test tomorrow. His intention is to get Sara to hurry up and pull herself together. In addition, there may be some boy-girl anxieties in the background, barely, if at all, conscious.

But Jason's sarcasm hurts Sara's feelings. She would like to be liked and admired even though she cannot seem to keep her Civil War battles straight. She thinks Jason meant to hurt her and put her down because he is mean and aggressive, and a boy. She masks her hurt feelings by calling Jason a creep. She wants to get even by making Jason feel small and ugly.

The situation has thus escalated; the original problem—covering the material in a limited time—has blown up into an unpleasant personal confrontation. Jason's semiserious, semiteasing behavior puts Sara on the defensive and she retaliates in full anger. Now he will have to defend himself. Under such circumstances, what can the teacher do? As you remember, the group we observed and described in the previous chapter was able to move past their quarrel fairly quickly, without intervention so that interference with the academic task was minimal. But suppose intervention is required. Then the teacher may decide simply to brush past the quarrel with a practical reminder of their task. On the other hand, he may decide it is time for these interpersonal difficulties to be faced directly. In this case he would attempt two things: (1) he would guide the children to an awareness of the effects they are having on one another, and (2) he would help them find better ways to express their feelings. His intervention might go something like this:

> "Let's look at what happened. Jason said this, Sara replied that. Jason, how were you feeling when you called Sara an idiot? Were you feeling mad?"
>
> "No . . . but she ought to hurry up, she ought to be organized by now."
>
> "So you were feeling impatient?"
>
> "Yes."
>
> "I bet you were also kind of worried about that test tomorrow."
>
> "Yes."
>
> "But did teasing help Sara straighten things out?"

Throughout this exchange, the teacher is helping Jason focus on *his* feelings and *his* behavior, and moving away from examining what is wrong with Sara. The teacher may sense the boy-girl issue but may want to save it for a later date when the children have more experience sharing their feelings and more confidence expressing themselves. He then returns to Sara and asks how she felt when Jason called her a name. She may reply that she wanted to punch him in the mouth (a quick and common translation of feeling into fantasy action), but with help she may admit to feeling anger and finally to feeling hurt. This is because the teacher has, at least for the moment, converted a win-lose atmosphere into one where it is safe to share feelings of vulnerability. The teacher does this by his attitude as much as anything else, by being caring and helpful and gentle. Intervention of an authoritarian nature ("Why did you do that? It's not nice. I'm ashamed of you. You know better.") has the opposite effect. Of course they know better, but they are caught in some difficult emotions and do not know what else to do.

One Solution: Learning to Make "I" Statements

Let's take a moment to clarify the theory underlying the mode of communication that we are recommending. As we all know, there are two ways we commonly use the word "feel." The first is really an opinion, my evaluation of *you*: I feel that you are an angry person, a wonderful fellow, or whatever. Feeling also has another, more basic meaning: I feel angry, sad, annoyed, happy I am expressing *my own* primary emotion. The focus is on "I," not "you" or "he" or "she." I am saying something about my own state rather than saying something judgmental about another person. It is feeling in this second sense that we think is the effective unit of communication for small-group problem solving, because it can be heard more easily by the recipient and so is more easily dealt with. It does not arouse defensiveness so it does not result in the other person wanting to run away or to fight back. When I say that I am feeling angry, I am expressing a fact. I know my feelings, there is no guesswork involved, no theories about your character (for example, "I feel frustrated" rather than "I feel you are irresponsible"). Now, if you want to interact with me, you will probably be interested in my feelings rather than defending yourself from a perceived attack. You may or may not want to determine whether or not you played any part in triggering my feelings but the focus is on the task at hand, since it would be useful (and perhaps necessary) to work this out before we can continue with our task. On the other hand, if I deliver a judgment about you instead of exposing my feelings, you will probably not be interested in anything but your own self-defense. Many older children are able to understand this. Younger children can simply learn to make "I" statements" rather than "you" statements, with the reasoning coming later.

To return to our classroom example, once the feelings have been clarified, the teacher might have to reassure students that it is all right to have "bad" feelings. He could point out that everyone does, and that it is legitimate to express anger or anxiety, but that there are ways to do it that are more constructive than others. If Sara had said outright: "I feel bad when you call me that" or "That makes me mad," Jason would have known immediately that his tactic of teasing was not having the effect he intended. Moreover, he would not have had to go on to prove he was not a creep. He could, of course, ignore Sara's protest. But at least he would have to ask himself, "Is that a good choice of behavior for what I want to accomplish?"

The dialogue described above is, of course, an idealized version of the process. It is usually not that quick or complete. But a hardworking group eventually reaches a point where interactions like this are neither impossible nor infrequent. One of the beauties of any small-group arrangement is that it provides the students with an opportunity for observing their own behavior as it affects others. It also provides opportunities for learning how to handle feelings of anger, impatience, shyness, or affection. Importantly, this learning occurs while the students are learning about the Civil War or the poetry of Emily Dickinson. The learning of communication skills is not a separate lesson in a jigsaw classroom. Rather, it enhances the mastery of the content at hand, increasing the usefulness and attentiveness of the human resources involved.[1]

THE NO PUT-DOWN CLASSROOM

Creating an environment that is free of put-downs is part of the classroom management strategy of an increasing number of teachers. It also sets the stage so that group members can approach difficulties as problems to solve rather than blaming each other. As a step toward creating a "put-down free zone" some teachers have used variations on the following: students are asked to write down all the put-downs they can think of, or the class as a whole brainstorms a list of put-downs. Once this is done, the teacher collects (or copies) the put-downs, places them in a receptacle, seals it, and disposes of it. The method of disposal varies, a bag can be simply tossed in the garbage, or a "coffin" can be given a proper burial with an appropriate ceremony attached. These exercises serve to call attention to what is inappropriate and later a student can be reminded with, "Why, I thought that comment was dead and buried."

---

[1] For a more detailed analysis of communication skills, see Chapter 8 in Elliot Aronson, *The Social Animal* (New York: W. H. Freeman, 1995).

PROBLEM: THE POOR READER

How do we help poor readers, children who may be reading one or several grade levels below their peers, and who, consequently, are suffering both in practical and emotional terms? As schools move away from tracking students, the reading ability of the children in a single classroom may vary considerably. In a jigsaw group, some group members will inevitably find themselves dependent for vital information on a student who, because of reading problems or for whom English is a second language, cannot easily get that information to them. The problem for relatively unskilled students is not only that they cannot read very well but also that they cannot hide the fact from their peers as they might have been able to do in a more traditional classroom. They are confronted with the impatience and unfavorable judgments of more skilled students. As a result, they are under pressure which potentially could inhibit their performance still further.

One Solution: Alternative Materials

There are several tactics a teacher can adopt in order to forestall such a destructive situation while at the same time increasing the flexibility of the learning environment. In a jigsaw group, anyone can make a useful contribution. For example, the slower reader may be given a drawing assignment, or the teacher can assign material of different reading levels to each group, making sure that the less accomplished readers get the least difficult material. Instead of copying a unit from a text where vocabulary and concepts are set at too high a grade level, a teacher can briefly summarize a portion of the material for a poor reader. Some of the material may also be recorded on cassettes, a task that might be assigned to quicker students to encourage in them a sense of responsibility toward their less skilled peers, while keeping them busy and challenged with an interesting, constructive task. Generally, recorded material is used in conjunction with, not instead of, written material in order to reinforce orally what the child is reading.

One Solution: Coaching

Another practice that has become common is that of student coaching with the higher-achieving students working directly with the slower students. This practice is more desirable than that of isolating a student with a tape recorder because it is yet another way to stress the development of interpersonal skills. The coaching teams are set up within each jigsaw group and serve to underscore its supportive values and the interdependency of the students. As we noted in our discussion of group composition, the benefits are mutual. The adept reader has the immediate, energizing reward of an image change—that is, he sees himself as a helper instead of as a hampered and bored student. The slower reader is being helped by someone who is more skilled but not perfect, a model within the limits of possible attainment, compared, for example, to the teacher, who is all-knowing. In our experience, this procedure opens slow readers to learning by reducing their need to feel intimidated and defensive. This in turn frees them to be more attentive and to take more risks in their learning, provided that their coaches have learned well their interpersonal skills.

When the jigsaw process is first getting underway, the teacher will probably be the one to suggest the coaching arrangement. Eventually, as cooperation becomes an established practice, the students themselves will make the choice to work in this manner. At first it is easier to imagine a faster student offering to help than it is to imagine a slower student taking the initiative to ask for that help. However, the kind of classroom the jigsaw teacher is developing is one where all the students realize that different levels of skills at any given moment are ordinary facts of life, a cause for neither shame nor vanity. The slower students or poorer readers often become quite accurate judges of what they can and cannot do and are not too embarrassed to ask for help when they need it.

Once the coaching team is set up, the teacher helps students make effective use of one another as resources. He shows them how to break a task into parts and also provides a structure for their interaction. For example, he might suggest that David first read the paragraph to Susan. Having heard the words and the rhythmical phrasing that serves to clarify content, Susan could then read the passage back. Then together they could decide on two important points and discuss how Susan is going to present them. As the teacher moves from group to group, he will want to be particularly attentive to how the coaching process is functioning. For example, is David getting impatient teaching down to Susan rather than working with her? The teacher may also ask students to comment on the process: Does David find that teaching the material helps him to learn it? How does Susan think the system is working for her? Does she have any suggestions for David that would enable him to be more helpful to her? The sooner the slower students are encouraged to state their own needs and opinions, the more confident they feel, the more they see that they have some control over their own learning.

Providing a variety of materials and arranging for student coaches are two strategies for helping poor readers that have worked in jigsaw classrooms, but of course they are not unique to the jigsaw approach; they can be employed in any classroom structure. Now let us look at a solution that is unique to the jigsaw procedure.

One Solution: The Expert Group

The expert group forms a basic part of the jigsaw structure. It encourages poorer readers or students for whom English is a second language to be helped by their peers, this time members of other groups who are responsible for learning the same material. The students in an expert group have a chance to hear the material read, are helped with the meaning of words, can share examples, and can try out their presentations. When the original jigsaw groups resume, even the slowest students have their sections fairly well planned and rehearsed. Through this procedure, they gain confidence. They begin to see themselves as useful members of a jigsaw group rather than as the "dummies."

PROBLEM: THE TROUBLEMAKER

Inevitably in almost any classroom there will be one or two students who, in relation to their classmates, are immature or recalcitrant; such students become known as "troublemakers." The same situation exists in a jigsaw classroom,. There will be students who simply will not work effectively in a group or who may even go so far as to sabotage efforts at cooperation by persistent attempts at mischief. Let's look at an example. Steve has a recurring game he likes to play: when Tametria is making her presentation, Steve makes the others laugh by mimicking her facial expressions and gestures. The group leader calls him on it, not for the first time. And, also not for the first time, Steve says, with wide-eyed innocence, that he wasn't doing anything—Tracy was. Steve's repeated "sneak and defense" behavior might be either an important survival tactic that he has developed at home or simply an attention-getting device. Whatever its cause, it is destructive to the group, and he is exerting a powerful disruptive influence. Moreover, he is not learning anything. It would be a mistake simply to thrust Steve into a jigsaw group without preparation.

One Solution: Special Handling

Students like Steve may need to work alone for a while under close adult supervision. Teachers we have worked with have made it clear to recalcitrant students that working in a jigsaw group is an opportunity to be earned, usually by making responsible decisions about a learning situation. For example, with teacher guidance, Steve may draw up a daily contract. It can be made clear to him at the outset that he is choosing to behave in a way that will exclude him from group work. First, he may simply be warned, but then the consequences of his behavior will be spelled out in his contract: He is choosing, through his behavior, to be excluded from the group—or to work his way back into the group. For example, Steve may agree (1) to learn the new words in the chapter summary and (2) to write a short paragraph on each explorer. It can be impressed upon him that these are the tasks to which he has committed himself. The teacher then begins to introduce him to cooperative activities. Perhaps he and another carefully chosen student are assigned to make a chart for the class. The point is that teachers find it wise to exclude and then bring the Steves in their classrooms step by step toward the goal of group participation. To leave them in a group and hope for the best can be disruptive to them and to other students.

PROBLEM: BOREDOM AND THE BRIGHT STUDENT

We are frequently asked what happens to the brightest students in the jigsaw situation. Don't they become impatient, bored, or resentful of the slower students? Boredom is not uncommon in elementary school regardless of the techniques being used, and it would be grossly misleading to imply that children working with the jigsaw process were never bored or impatient. While todays teachers are better trained than their predecessors, they must also contend with the higher expectancies and the lower thresholds for boredom that typify most young children. No matter how gifted the teacher, how exciting the subject matter, how engrossing the activities, the classroom lacks the excitement, variety, and pace of children's entertainment options. Moreover, because their minds are so quick, bright students tend to be among the most easily bored if events are moving too slowly for them.

One other point is relevant in this context. In developing the jigsaw method special pains were taken to minimize conflict and/or resentment among students. For this reason, we designed jigsaw so that children would learn new material in a cooperative fashion but they would be tested individually and receive individual scores rather than an average of the group score. Thus bright students have the opportunity to score individually; in no way can a score be diminished by the exam performance of a less gifted student. This aspect of jigsaw has proven itself to be congenial with the desires of most students as well as those of their parents.

While jigsaw has proven to be one good way to reduce boredom, there are other ways. Indeed, one surefire way any teacher can reduce boredom is to refuse to stick to one method, whether it is competitiveness, individually guided instruction, multimedia presentations, or cooperative learning techniques including jigsaw.

One Solution: Peer Tutoring

While it may be impossible to eliminate boredom from the school experience, teachers who have used the jigsaw technique report a great deal *less* boredom among their students than is the case in a more competitive classroom atmosphere. Our data support this observation: children in jigsaw classes do like school better than children in the control classes, and this is true for the bright students as well as the slower students. There is an old adage, *docemur docendo* (he who teaches learns). This is clearly the case in the jigsaw situation. Teaching can be an exciting change of pace for students. It frees them from being a more or less passive receptacles of information and allows them the opportunity to try a new skill. Not only does this almost certainly reduce boredom but if introduced properly it can also reduce the impatience that bright students otherwise experience when slower students are experiencing difficulty. By developing the mind-set of "teacher," the bright students can turn what might have been a boring waste of time into an exciting challenge. And, as previously reported, this challenge produces not only psychological benefits but more thorough learning as well.

One Solution: Using Your Bored Bright Student

Many classrooms have students who are chronically absent yet when they are in class they need (perhaps more than most) to be included in the jigsaw groups. The bored bright student might be able to serve as a "generalist" for the group and possibly for the class. Their abilities make it likely that they would already know the material and this would give them something active and useful to do.

PROBLEM: OBTAINING AND DEVELOPING INSTRUCTIONAL MATERIALS

Perhaps the most difficult problem new jigsaw teachers face is that of obtaining and developing appropriate instructional materials. The usual curriculum material must be divided into segments for the students to share. Some assignments have to be created from various resources, others can simply be reproduced from texts.

One Solution: Sharing Resources

Nearly all books on cooperative learning include sections on jigsaw and devising lessons in a wide variety of subjects. There are even a few books that focus on jigsaw activities alone (see Coelho, Winer, and Olson 1989). With jigsaw, everything must be transferred to cards that can be handed out once class begins. This requires time, which is always a precious commodity to the teacher. More specifically, it requires the *efficient use* of time. When we get rushed, we tend to plan less and be less systematic while just the opposite behavior is most efficient.

As mentioned before, the ideal time for teachers to prepare curriculum is when they are under no pressure to teach it, such as during vacations, and this is when most teachers do it. When time pressures are off, the creativity of the task can be enjoyed. Once these plans and materials are developed, teachers can share units with one another. When colleagues share prepared jigsaw lessons, they not only save time but also model cooperation for their students. A team of teachers not only decreases the workload but also eliminates the loneliness that can develop when one is attempting something new.

There may be instances when the students themselves can help in the physical preparation of a unit, transferring materials to cards, cutting copied material into strips, and gathering illustrations. In some classrooms, a jigsaw group can be assigned the entire responsibility for a unit. The students devise the assignments, decide how to divide and distribute the reading material, and create questions and exercises. This kind of organizing activity is an effective way of learning material as teachers well know from their own experience when, for example, they discover the Civil War they have managed to avoid for a lifetime is coming up in the next chapter of the seventh-grade text. However, to be able to shoulder such responsibility in a cooperative effort, the students should have some experience in the group process techniques of jigsawing. Thus a unit on curriculum planning might best be left until spring.

Finally, most school districts have sponsored in-services on cooperative learning. The curriculum supervisor of a district will often know what group materials are available for each subject and level.

PROBLEM: OTHER SCHOOL PERSONNEL

Most teachers learn quickly that cooperative learning is noisy. Picture this scene. Children are scattered around the room, with everybody talking at once. Chaos. And the principal walks in. What is she likely to conclude? That the teacher must be an undisciplined person, unskilled, ineffective? How can children learn anything in such a noisy atmosphere? Or perhaps, she thinks, the teacher does not care, is sacrificing academics and good behavior to some vague ideal of spontaneity.

Such might also be the thoughts of a nonjigsaw teacher upon observing a jigsaw classroom for the first time. The jigsaw classroom is noisy but as most experienced teachers know, there is noise that is just noise, and there is the kind of noise that is the sound of learning and living. Outsiders to the jigsaw and other cooperative learning methods may believe they are witnessing chaos when in reality they are observing creative energy released by a carefully planned structure, not youthful energy combating structure.

One Solution: Share Knowledge

Jigsaw teachers have found it useful to prepare their supervisors and colleagues for their classroom innovations. Most educators today have at least been exposed to cooperative learning ideas and techniques so explaining what you are up to is no longer difficult. Teachers have learned that it facilitates understanding when they remind the other professionals in their environment that cooperative learning encourages student responsibility. The goals of jigsaw teachers are no different from those of their colleagues. Some teachers ask their colleagues to sit in on a jigsaw group and then share their opinions as to the effectiveness of the technique in teaching the content material. All too often, classrooms and their teachers are isolated units in the school. In some schools teachers are colleagues only insofar as they hold the same degrees and work in the same building. For a jigsaw teacher to open her method to discussion gives some substance to the word "colleague." We provide a step-by-step description of a one-day in-service workshop in Chapter 8 so that the experience of jigsaw and the development of its component skills is available to everyone. Teachers are strongly encouraged to participate in such workshops in school teams, perhaps grade level teams. They will then have the support they need on-site as well as other teachers with whom to share the burden of preparing materials.

Students too must be able to articulate class objectives to outsiders, particularly to those parents who say, "That's not the way we did things in my day!" To this end, teachers and students often develop a routine for welcoming visitors and showing them around and explaining solutions to parents having such concerns as grading and the appropriateness of jigsaw for their particular child.

PROBLEM: MAINTAINING A COOPERATIVE SPIRIT

There are times even among experienced jigsaw groups when the cooperative spirit seems to dissipate and the students lose interest. The jigsaw teacher is concerned with keeping alive a more enjoyable, productive, and supportive mood.

One Solution: Additional Team-building

We mentioned earlier that a change of routine by meeting in the expert groups can be helpful. In addition, one fifth-grade teacher begins each new unit (for which new groups are usually formed) with team-building exercises, and once every few weeks begins the jigsaw hour with some variation on the Broken Squares exercises described earlier. This takes only five minutes, at the end of which time the students are ready to work more closely with each other. Other teachers have discovered stories or parables that inspire their students and build cooperative spirit; storytelling can teach and relax at the same time.

PROBLEM: TEACHER DISCOURAGEMENT

We have been concentrating thus far on how to help the students. But what about the teacher? Who helps the helper? As you know, even under the most ideal circumstances, teaching is not an easy, stress-free vocation. Most teachers get discouraged for any number of reasons during the course of a school year. This is especially true when they are initiating a new method—the pressure of new responsibilities, the insecurity of not knowing in advance what will and will not work. The advice we are about to discuss can be used effectively by any teacher using almost any technique, but the jigsaw teachers we have worked with have found it particularly helpful.

One Solution: Teacher Support Teams

Guilt and anxiety are feelings reported by most skilled teachers, reflected in their tendency to demand perfection of themselves 100 percent of the time. They fall into a slump, the bad day of week is all their fault, they are not reaching one or two students who are having trouble. As we all know, when we feel discouraged, we feel better if we can talk about it. It may seem functional for a teacher to be able to let off steam in the staff room. Unfortunately, this is not a helpful tactic if it stimulates a general "gripe" session. For example, a teacher who is momentarily discouraged may mention a student who was very disruptive that particular morning, which may elicit sympathy and support or perhaps a volley of stories that begin, "If you think that's bad, let me tell you the trouble *I'm* having." After a session of this sort, when the teachers return to their classrooms, they have not solved their problem and are likely to feel even worse. Much more helpful than this type of commiseration is a group of colleagues that meet as part of a support system. In our experience with teachers using the jigsaw technique, those who were happiest and got the most out of it were the ones who were able to form a group for mutual support and consultation. Members not only support each other emotionally, but encourage rational problem solving. This creates norms to give teachers energy and direction and to devise a systematic method for exploring new alternatives. Being a good consultant is itself a skill, but one that can be easily acquired.

One Solution: Peer Consultation

The effective consultant hears fellow teachers out, listens supportively, and then asks the kinds of questions that will clarify issues and generate possible solutions. Sometimes discouraged teachers state explicitly the kind of help they are looking for. For example, a teacher might say he is in a slump and simply wants to unburden himself. He asks a colleague to listen for a few minutes and say back to him what she thinks she hears him saying. Even if he does not quite know what he wants, it can be very helpful to have the gist of his own words played back by a consultant. This helps him think the problem through. The next step may be to go on to consider the questions that he could usefully ask himself in order to begin shaping a solution. Here is an illustration: Carol is a student who is falling behind. Her teacher is particularly upset because Carol had started the year full of excitement and hope; this year, in this classroom, she was really going to work hard and learn something. Now the teacher believes he has failed her somehow. Has he? While his feelings are painful and worthy of sympathy, the question about his failure is not a particularly fruitful one in practical terms. So after acknowledging his feelings, the consultant might encourage him to ask himself: What specific learning problems does Carol have? What does the record say? What do I know about her attitudes? How could the technique we are using (jigsaw or whatever) be affecting her difficulties? Such questions developed and examined with trusted colleagues will benefit Carol. And, very importantly, because these questions are infused with practical energy, because they reflect the teacher's power to analyze and understand a problem and to be of specific use, they benefit him by allaying his fears and combating discouragement: there *is* something he can do. In sum, while a support system gives a teacher some opportunity to vent feelings and to have a sense of being heard, most of the time is spent on specifically defining a problem and thinking about different ways to solve it.

CHAPTER 6

PUTTING ALL THE PIECES TOGETHER

In the preceding chapters, we have presented an occasional example to illustrate a point, but we have not offered a complete picture of a jigsaw class at work. There has been more tell than show. We now would like to describe one-hour in a real jigsaw classroom, Ms. Taylors sixth-grade class.

MS. TAYLOR'S CLASSROOM

Ms. Taylor is an experienced teacher who has been using the jigsaw approach for two years; the class is a model one. As with ever)' successful enterprise, to develop a smoothly functioning jigsaw classroom required hard work and experience. In their early stages few classrooms proceed as well as Ms. Taylor's. But her class is not an ideal version of how a jigsaw classroom *might* function; rather it is an accurate picture of how a very good jigsaw class *does* function.

Ms. Taylor welcomed us into her class and informed us that the students were about to begin an hour of social studies. They had been assigned to new groupings a week earlier when they began a unit on the colonial period. We learned that, as in many classes, students functioned at varied reading levels. For example, three or four were reading at only the first- or second-grade level. As was the case in other classes in this school, even children with severe learning problems were maintained in regular classes. Ms. Taylor told us that this class had been using the jigsaw approach for three months and that the students had learned to work together very well. She also said that the students were accustomed to having observers and our presence would not disturb them.

Ms. Taylor then rang a bell and when the students were quiet, she introduced us. She asked the students to get into their groups and to spend five minutes reviewing before outlining the agenda for this period. For each six-person group, the member whose turn it was to be the recorder got the group's folder from a box. In the group nearest us, Kevin returned with the folder for his group; Lisa, the team leader, asked him to read the brief notes that described where they had stopped the previous day. She then addressed a question to the entire group: "What are we going to do today?" After the group developed the hour's agenda, Lisa asked Kevin to read the previous day's group process evaluation cards. Kevin commented that the group needed to improve its ability to stay on task and not get sidetracked. He also cautioned the group that it appeared they were falling behind and would not be ready to be tested on the material they had agreed to study. With an impatient look at Amy, who was not listening, Kevin concluded by saying that Amy had agreed to pay attention. Amy looked a little embarrassed and annoyed but did not change her behavior; that is, she continued to look inattentive for the next ten minutes, at which time Lisa reminded her to listen.

On this particular day, Ms. Taylor rang her bell after the first ten minutes in order to allow each group to get a sense of what the other groups were doing. Each group was asked to describe its academic goals and to list what materials it had already finished. Each group leader asked someone from his group to report. For example, Ms. Taylor called on Lisa, who nodded to Jon. Jon reported that they had finished studying the economic conditions in the colonial period and had given the material to another group along with suggestions on how to use it. Today they were going to start studying colonial religions, having just received the materials from another group. We noted that even though at any one time the groups may have been working on different topics, they seemed quite willing to help each other.

For the colonial unit Ms. Taylor had prepared jigsaw activity cards for each topic.[1] Lisa passed a card to Mark, Kevin, Amy, Nicole, and Jon, and to herself. The cards suggested ways that each student could help focus discussion on important issues and directed the student to additional resource information, such as reference books and, for the students who had difficulty reading, to tapes. Performance objectives accompanied the material to help students know specifically what must be presented. For example, the student whose topic was Puritanism was given a card with this instruction on it: "Each member of your team should be able to name two colonies in which Puritanism was found." Since each student was responsible for teaching different information, each knew that the others were relying on him for his part. If group members did not teach their individual parts well, the group as a whole would not be able to meet its performance objectives. The group members realized that in order to help each member teach well, they needed to listen carefully and ask good questions.

Ms. Taylor had copied the resource material that accompanied each card so that the students could promptly begin work on their presentations. Since Amy was the fastest worker, she helped Jon, who was having difficulty with

---

[1] If the teacher had not prepared these materials, we might have seen the group leader dividing up the tasks among the members (e.g., one religion for each student to research), and then the members would go to available resource materials such as social studies texts.

some of the words on the sheets.[2] After ten minutes, Lisa interrupted to see how much more time they would need; they decided to begin discussion in five minutes. The students continued reading over their material, jotting down notes on essential points they wanted to teach the group, and thinking of ways to raise the discussion questions suggested on the activity cards. After five minutes had passed, Lisa called the group back together. They decided to try limiting themselves to 10 or 15 minutes on each topic in order to finish the following day. Nicole's presentation was to be the first piece in their jigsaw puzzle of information. Her topic was "religious persecution" and she began by asking her groupmates to close their eyes, as was suggested on the activity card. She told them to imagine they deeply believed in a religion, yet the police would not let them go to their church. They were told to try to experience such things as living in England three centuries ago . . . being beaten and put in jail. . . suffering economic losses . . . their children being taught another re-ligion in school . . . deciding to leave . . . sorrow at leaving . . . the tough, per-ilous trip across the ocean . . . a difficult start. . . hardships, but also schools where their children learned their own religion . . . living, by choice, with peo-ple who shared their beliefs, and so on. Although Jon and Amy seemed to have trouble paying attention, the fantasy appeared to help the others prepare for the discussion. Nicole asked them to open their eyes, and began to tell them about the persecution in Europe and why many people gave up so much to come settle a new land. She read some questions from the activity card: "If these people gave up so much to be able to practice their own religion and to have it taught at school, do you think they would want to let other religious views be taught in their schools? If they believed dancing was bad, do you think they would pass laws against dancing? If they believed everyone should go to their church, do you think they would pass laws to make people go? After all, they had given up a lot to live in just the way they wanted." Most of the students nodded yes. Then she read the next question, "But what if you and a friend didn't believe in Puritanism? Should you have to learn that at school, or go to a Puritan church?"

A lively discussion ensued, covering the topics suggested by the questions on the activity card. We were very impressed to see the amount of understand-ing the students had of what it was actually like for settlers such as the Puri-tans, of what issues they had faced and how they actually had dealt with them.

The students were so involved in the discussion that Lisa needed to inter-rupt in order to remind them of their time limits. The group quickly reached a consensus to extend their allotted time and resumed the discussion. Jon be-came rather excited and told Lisa she was "stupid" for saying that she thought

---

[2] If all the groups in the class had been working on the same material, we would probably have seen one representative from each group form a temporary counterpart group for 15 minutes.

that the Puritans ought to be able to force everyone to go to their church. Lisa quickly retaliated by saying that Jon was too "dumb" and "weird" to know anything about religion. At this point Amy interrupted and said, "Wait a minute! You know we're not supposed to call anyone names. Stick to the topic. Anyway, Ms. Taylor said there were no right or wrong answers, so quit acting like know-it-alls." Even though Amy herself was calling people names, the group did get back on the subject. They decided to move on to the next topic after a brief discussion of the final question: "In our group, do we ever persecute each other or force our beliefs on each other as happened to the colonists? Why might that happen here?"

Although most of our attention as observers had been focused on the students, we also were noticing some interesting things about Ms. Taylor's behavior toward the groups. She was moving from group to group, checking the quality of discussion and behavior. Sometimes she merely listened to a group. More often she knelt beside the leader to ask a question or make a suggestion. In particular, when she came to our group she quietly mentioned to Lisa, the leader, that it did not look as if everyone were participating. (In fact, we had observed that Mark had said nothing and his chair was pulled back slightly outside the circle.) Ms. Taylor asked Lisa what the group might do to help create an atmosphere where everybody would feel able to participate. After Ms. Taylor left, we noted that Lisa interrupted by saying, "Let's wait a second. Are we helping everyone to say whatever they're thinking?"

Kevin responded sharply, "Mark's been off in the clouds again. Why don't you talk like everyone else?"

Amy said, "Quit picking on him. If you weren't talking all the time, maybe he could say something!"

Lisa interrupted to help the group figure out how to make it easier for Mark to share his ideas. They decided to pause briefly between people's comments to make sure that others would have a chance to add their own ideas. They also encouraged Mark to say whatever he wanted, and Lisa and Jon told him that whenever he had talked in the past, they had liked his ideas.

The group we were observing was in the middle of a second lesson when Ms. Taylor interrupted the class to announce the end of the group session. She asked them to jot down how far they had gotten on their agenda and then to spend the last five minutes with their group process cards. Each person filled out a card, using several criteria to evaluate how he worked in the group that day. Lisa then asked the group as a whole to rate itself in several categories and, using these ratings, they discussed how they could work more effectively the following day.

ANALYSIS

While this was a rather typical sample of a good, experienced jigsaw group at work, the behavior of the children was far from perfect group behavior. Amy, for example, was inattentive, perhaps bored. While we cannot be certain after only a brief observation, we would guess that her lack of attentiveness might be attributable to the fact that things were moving too slowly for her. If this were the reason, the group leader or the teacher would want to focus on this problem. One solution would be to get Amy involved as a teacher of the slower students in her group. The goal would be to change her perception of her role from bored student for whom things are going too slowly to the role of active helper. Then Amy's lack of attentiveness should decrease and her involvement increase.

While Kevin noticed Amy's lack of attentiveness, his mild annoyance was communicated in a punitive manner. As Lisa becomes more familiar with her leadership role, under the tutelage of Ms. Taylor, she will learn to handle such a situation more productively. Similarly, as she becomes more adept, she will be able to bring quieter students like Mark into the discussion in a tactful way before his inactivity becomes a source of embarrassment to him. Moreover, Kevin will probably learn to express his feelings without attacking others.

How will he learn? And how could the squabbling and name-calling which occurred in this group be reduced? One advantage of the small group is that it occasionally allows the focus to be on the squabble itself, which can be a means of helping children practice the skills they are developing to facilitate better interpersonal relations—that is, about how to help children communicate with one another more effectively and in a less disruptive manner.

CHAPTER 7

RESEARCH ON JIGSAW

We began our research evaluating the effectiveness of the jigsaw technique some 25 years ago, at the time we entered our first classroom in the Austin, Texas, public school system. Since that time, we have trained teachers to use jigsaw in every section of this country and in several foreign countries. In many of these locales, we had the opportunity to replicate our initial scientific research, demonstrating over and over again the effectiveness of the jigsaw technique. On the following pages, we will confine our discussion primarily to the initial research project, with only occasional reference to some of the subsequent replications.

Before we begin this discussion, it might be prudent to raise a fundamental question: Why do formal research, anyway? After -all, experienced teachers do not need complex statistical analyses, charts, graphs, or numerical tables in order to assess the viability of an instructional technique. Teachers are sensitive to subtle changes in the classroom atmosphere and to relatively minor improvements in the performance and attitude of individual students. In the early 1970s, when we first instituted the jigsaw technique in Austin, some rather dramatic events occurred in the classrooms that convinced the participating teachers that jigsaw was a useful, powerful strategy. It was gratifying to us that the teachers who experimented with jigsaw were sold on it long before we were. As rather stodgy scientific investigators, we needed to collate and analyze our data before we could be sure. But while we were still in the process of our statistical analyses, almost all the teachers in the initial sample were enthusiastically reporting classroom anecdotes and success stories to us.

For example, Mr. T, a teacher in Austin, told us of a discovery made by the brightest student in his class: "You know, Mr. T, I used to think that Paul was dumb—but now I know that he really tries."

A short time later, a teacher from Santa Cruz, California, told us about Charles, a student who came to the class after the start of the school year. He was slow academically and had difficulty paying attention and staying in his seat. He also had trouble on the playground. She reported to us about what happened when the jigsaw technique was initiated: "From the very beginning, jigsaw was perfect for Charles. Even though his reading skills were underdeveloped, he learned the material through listening after one session in his expert group. Since jigsaw involves some movement and a lot of conversation, I rarely had to go hunting for Charles in the halls. Jigsawing gave him a chance to be the focal point of at least five other students' attention. . . . Anything that involved strictly reading and writing, or even whole class simulation games (where he would always want to be center of attention), simply wouldn't work with Charles. But because of jigsaw, Charles and I developed a good relationship." Other teachers reported similar success with difficult students. One story involved Bill, a student who was seen in his other classes as a clown. By putting him in a team situation (thus separating him from some of his closest friends), he was forced into working with a completely new group of people. "We discovered a great leadership quality that had been hidden before." Another student, Peter, was described as a fair student with difficulty reading, which resulted in low self-esteem. His teacher offered this report: "Peter was extremely worried about the effect each quiz would have on his grade. His first question was always, 'What if I flunk?'" She went on, "Being a member of a jigsaw team really helped him deal with that fear. The other members of the team helped him learn the material and gave him support and the assurance that he would not fail."

In another school, several of the teachers told us proudly that their pupils' change in attitude generalized to other classes throughout the school. For example, both the music and physical education teachers complimented the jigsaw teachers on their students' behavior, mentioning that the students as a whole had become noticeably more cooperative and considerate. Since the music and P.E. teachers were not involved in the jigsaw project and were not even aware that anything different was happening in the regular classrooms, it was particularly rewarding to the jigsaw teachers that a major change had been discerned. These are the things that matter: changes in student behavior, attitudes, and performance.

With testimony like this to fall back on, why should we bother to do systematic research? Isn't first-hand experience all that matters? Not quite. It is conceivable that individual teachers, because of their commitment to the project and general agreement with our goals, may have done some subliminal editing—emphasizing positive incidents and relegating negative ones to the back burners of their memory. Moreover, it is possible that exceptional progress can indeed occur in a few classrooms, but it may be due to special circumstances that have little or nothing to do with the jigsaw technique itself, marvelous weather or an upcoming holiday. In these cases it would be erroneous to conclude that the jigsaw technique is effective when perhaps it is not.

For these reasons, it is essential to have independent, well-controlled research data. Although in the technical reports of this research the focus was on numbers and statistics, we hoped not to lose sight of the fact that learning is accomplished by individuals. The goal of this research was to determine systematically whether or not jigsaw is valuable in the classroom.

The research on jigsaw groups grew, in part, out of our ideas about education. However, no research project comes entirely from the heads of those who design it. In the first chapter, we talked about how the concern about the extreme consequences of competitiveness—especially as it was then manifested in newly desegregated schools—led to the development of the jigsaw technique. While this is accurate, it is also true that many of the ideas were influenced by the research that other scientists have conducted while exploring the place of cooperation and competition in the classroom. Just as understandably, those classroom needs are the primary interest on the part of teachers hoping for more useful information from researchers.

One of the major purposes for our own research was to fill both needs simultaneously. Researchers must design careful scientific experiments so that they can assess whether or not their techniques work. It was our aim to be as meticulous as possible so that the results of our work could bear up under the careful scrutiny. At the same time, we made every effort to develop a program and a set of techniques that teachers could apply in the classroom as well as explain them to other teachers. Thus, although we were interested in the scientific results of this study, we were equally interested in planting the seed of jigsaw groups and helping them grow and spread from classroom to classroom.

JIGSAW PILOT STUDY

We combined two successful techniques, cooperation and peer-teaching, in our research. This was done by putting students in cooperative (jigsaw) groups where each student would have the opportunity to be both the teacher and the learner. To see if this was feasible, a two-week exploratory study was conducted before launching the full-scale investigation.

In the initial pilot study, students in two fifth-grade classrooms were divided into learning groups of five to six students. Half of the groups were taught by a teacher, the other half were cooperative groups organized in the jigsaw manner. In the latter groups, the assignment was divided into pieces, like a jigsaw puzzle, and each student was given a segment of the assignment that no other student had. Each student taught his or her piece of information to the other students in the group. That way, each student had to learn what each other member of the group knew in order to learn the entire lesson for the day.

Liking Ratings

At several points in the study, the students liking for one another was measured to see if it changed as a result of the type of learning groups. Just prior to the beginning of the study, there were no differences in liking ratings expressed by the students for their group members. However, at the halfway point in this study, members of the jigsaw groups liked each other more than members of the traditional teacher-taught groups did.

At this point the teacher-taught groups were placed into the jigsaw environment—that is, they became cooperative groups. At the end of the study, liking ratings were again the same among all groups: liking ratings among those formerly teacher-taught (now jigsaw) groups were now as high as the liking ratings among the original jigsaw groups. We concluded that the jigsaw technique had caused an increase in liking within the groups. Further, it seemed clear that simply working in small learning groups was not sufficient to increase liking among members of the groups. It was not until the teacher-taught groups became jigsaw groups that the liking ratings for members of those groups increased.

Encouraged by the results of this small study, we launched a full-scale project in collaboration with the participating teachers. Remember the context: We were trying to solve a problem concerning the lack of success with racial integration in the classroom. At that time, classroom atmosphere was on our minds.

Hypotheses

1. Students in jigsaw groups will like their groupmates more than the rest of their classmates.
2. Compared to students in traditional classrooms, students in jigsaw classrooms will
   a. like school more.
   b. show a greater increase in self-esteem.
   c. show a decrease in feelings of competitiveness.
   d. believe more that they can learn from other children.

THE FULL-SCALE JIGSAW RESEARCH

With so much previous research pointing to the usefulness of cooperation in the classroom and with the results of the pilot jigsaw study, why was anything else needed? Wasn't there already sufficient proof that a cooperative technique like jigsaw groups work? The teachers and students in the pilot study liked the jigsaw groups and there were positive effects on students' liking for one another. Why not simply implement jigsaw and let more students benefit? At this stage, research may seem like a needless waste of time. And indeed this is exactly what happens with many educational innovations.

The most reliable way to ensure an unbiased evaluation is to conduct some kind of carefully controlled research. By carefully controlled, we mean primarily that (1) the questions to be answered through the research have been formulated beforehand and (2) the questionnaires or other research instruments used are constructed so that the data from persons experiencing the new method can be compared with data (also from the same instruments) from persons who are not experiencing the new method. This comparison is the key and it is important to find an appropriate comparison group. Comparison groups or control groups are used in all types of scientific research. In the jigsaw study, the control group consisted of classrooms where students were not divided into jigsaw groups; the teachers did most of the teaching and the atmosphere was that found in normally competitive classrooms.

Since the control classes were an essential part of the study, the control teachers were selected as carefully as the jigsaw teachers. It was important that both groups of teachers be competent and highly committed to their methods of teaching. One possibility would have been to select a control group from among the teachers who had volunteered to try jigsaw. However, since the teachers were all volunteering to learn a new technique, we assumed that they might not be strongly committed to their present style of teaching and that they might not be motivated to try very hard if asked to continue in the same old way; we wanted good teachers who also liked what they were doing. Since we wanted to have control teachers and jigsaw teachers from the same schools and the same grade levels, we asked the jigsaw teachers to give us the names of grade level colleagues whom they considered to be as competent as they themselves were but who were committed to and happy with more typical teaching techniques. These teachers were then asked to participate in the study as controls. To have secured control teachers who were less committed or less effective than the jigsaw teachers would have rendered the control groups useless for comparison.

Measuring Liking for School

Recall that the first hypothesis stated that students in jigsaw classes would like school more than students in control classes. Since things had been arranged so that these two types of classes were as similar as possible, except that the jigsaw classes contained cooperative groups, we knew that any differences in the findings could be attributed to the effect of the cooperative groups.

To assess the effect of the jigsaw groups, we designed a 22-item questionnaire to measure students' attitudes toward school and toward themselves. A second questionnaire was designed to measure students' liking for each of their classmates. The two questionnaires were administered at the beginning of the study, to measure attitudes and liking before the study began, and at the end of six weeks to see if there had been any change.

This was done in both the control and the jigsaw classrooms using a standardized script. For the attitude questionnaire, each of the 22 questions was read aloud twice, and students were asked to indicate their answers by marking one of seven boxes of increasing size under each question. Accompanying each box was a verbal description of the meaning of that box. The figure below shows how the first question looked.

"How much do you like school this year?"

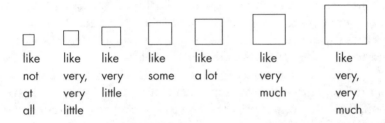

like	like	like	like	like	like	like
not	very,	very	some	a lot	very	very,
at	very	little			much	very
all	little					much

This way of presenting the questions was helpful for students who had difficulty[7] in reading. If students did not like school at all, they checked the smallest box; if they did not dislike school entirely they checked the next-to-smallest box, and so on, up to the largest box, which they checked if they liked school very much. Thus the boxes provided a "picture" of the increasing degree of feeling represented by the verbal labels underneath each box.

Measuring Liking for Others

We considered a variety of methods that would enable us to measure the students' liking for others. Teachers had advised against asking students simply to tell us whom they did and did not like. This method would have done away with the complexity and labor imposed by other methods, but teachers feared that asking children to state liking and disliking outright might create discomfort and hurt feelings among the students. We agreed with them and decided that a method involving a fantasy boat trip to an island was a reasonable way to secure sociometric data, pleasant for the students while yielding valuable data.

Specifically, the students were asked to imagine taking a trip to an exciting island with all their classmates. They had to make the trip in a small boat, and although the boat could carry only a few classmates at a time, eventually, with enough trips, the entire class could come to the island. Each student was given a roster listing all the people in the class and was asked to place a number from one to seven beside each name. The numbers indicated how soon they wanted each classmate to join them on the island. Seven was assigned to those class-mates the student wanted *most* to be with and who could go over on the first boatload. Classmates given the number six would be able to go on the second boatload, and so on.

We did not want students in the jigsaw classes to realize that the question-naires were related in any way to the fact that they were working in groups because we were afraid that this knowledge might affect the way they answered the questions, thus distorting our results. For this reason, students in both the jigsaw and control classes were told that the questionnaires were part of a study of the entire school system and that fifth-grade students in many other schools were also answering the same questionnaires. Finally, the persons adminis-tering the questionnaires took special care not to show the students' answers to their teachers. Accordingly, students in both jigsaw and control classes could be assured that their answers were confidential.

In order to be certain that any changes in attitudes or liking were due to the effect of the jigsaw groups, it was important that experimental conditions were different. First, the control teachers were asked to agree to refrain from breaking their class into small groups, and especially not into cooperative ones, during the course of the research. Second, in order to ensure that the jigsaw technique was used similarly in all jigsaw classes, a series of workshops was conducted to provide jigsaw teachers with identical training. Teachers in the control classes did not attend these workshops. Therefore, any differences found in student attitude between the two types of classes could be attributed to the effect of the jigsaw groups.

The first workshop lasted five days and was held just before school began. It was designed so that teachers learned how to use the jigsaw method by ex-periencing it themselves. They learned skills to help the jigsaw groups function smoothly and to view their role in the jigsaw method as that of group facili-tator rather than as primary provider of information, all concepts we have pre-sented in this book. In addition, teachers had to adapt their own curriculum material to the jigsaw method and devise strategies to help students with spe-cific learning or behavior problems that might develop in their groups. During the following months, several half-day workshops were held to provide addi-tional training and to allow teachers to interact with and help one another.

Back in the classroom, the jigsaw teachers were asked to assign their stu-dents to small groups that were as heterogeneous as possible. The reasons for this approach, some of which have been discussed previously, also helped with the research design: we wanted to be sure that our data were generalizable to all students. For example, if many groups had consisted of only boys, our data would have been limited primarily to groups consisting of all boys. Accordingly, we asked teachers to distribute differences in ethnicity, academic ability, and sex as evenly as possible among groups. Also, students who were either close friends or bitter enemies were not placed together. Groups usually consisted of five to six members and generally met for 40 to 45 minutes a day, at least three days a week.

Of course, simply putting students in the same small group was no guarantee that they would be able to work together effectively from the very beginning. To facilitate the transition to jigsaw learning, teachers led their groups in a series of short team-building exercises (described previously) before the students actually began to work together. The exercises as a whole provided students with experiences to help them focus upon skills that would be important to their success in jigsaw groups. These exercises were used only at the beginning of the groups, before actual group work began, as a way to lay the foundation for effective group functioning.

In order to reinforce these skills and help the students improve their group's functioning, the last five minutes of each group period were set aside for group processing. During this time, students used guidelines developed during team-building to assess how well their group had functioned that day. As discussed earlier, these guidelines focused on what group members might do in order to help one another communicate and learn more effectively. After filling out checklists for individual members as well as for the group as a whole, groupmates would discuss their checklists, pinpoint their trouble areas, and reach decisions on what they would try to do differently next time.

During this processing, the teacher moved from group to group in order to demonstrate ways to give noncritical, constructive feedback about how an individual or the group as a whole was behaving. The goal of all this was to increase the students' awareness of how they could improve their functioning as a learning group.

SUMMARY OF RESULTS

We have already described a typical jigsaw session. Here is a brief overview:

Every member of every group was responsible for learning all the curriculum material, *but individual students had direct access to only their part of the material—the part they were to teach others.* Since they had to depend on groupmates for access to the rest of the material, it became essential for all groupmates to do a good job of communicating their parts of the material. Along with that, students had to do a good job of listening. If material being shared was not clear, groupmates had to learn to ask the student to clarify the material. Moreover, it was functional to learn to ask in ways that would help the student do a better job of communicating rather than to be destructive or intimidating. In essence, the students in each group were putting their knowledge together a piece at a time, each student contributing a piece of the jigsaw puzzle of material.

Following is a summary of the findings:

1. Students in jigsaw classrooms increased their liking for their groupmates without decreasing their liking for other people in their classroom.
2. Students in jigsaw classrooms tended to increase their liking for school to a greater extent than did children in traditional classrooms. Not only did they *say* that they liked school better, but their rate of absenteeism decreased markedly and was significantly lower than students in the more traditional classrooms.
3. Students in jigsaw classrooms increased their self-esteem, decreased their competitiveness, and viewed their classmates as learning resources; similar results were not found among students in traditional classrooms.
4. African-American and Latino students in jigsaw classrooms learned the material significantly better than their counterparts in traditional classrooms (as measured by objective test results).
5. White students performed as well in the jigsaw groups as in the traditional groups.
6. Students in jigsaw classrooms showed a greater ability than those in competitive classrooms to put themselves in the role of another person, even outside of the school environment.

Taken together, these results showed that a strong, positive pattern of behaviors, feelings, and abilities could be attributed to jigsaw groups. Now the details.

THE LIKING MEASURE

This measure was used to find out how much students liked one another and what effect, if any, the jigsaw groups had upon this liking. We had predicted that liking for one another would increase within jigsaw classrooms. In addition, we were interested in how well the students liked people who were not in their group.

Before we examine the results, let's take a closer look at this hypothesis. Imagine a situation where all five members of a group have grown to like one another very well during their six weeks of learning together. Suppose also that these five students had become such a tight-knit group that they no longer studied or played much with classmates that they had been friends with before the groups. Worse still, suppose that these five buddies actually came to dislike the other students. In such a situation the jigsaw groups would clearly have had an impact, but it would not be entirely beneficial, to say the least. Therefore two types of liking scores were calculated for each student in the jigsaw classes. One represented the average of the liking ratings individual students gave their groupmates, and the other represented the average of the liking ratings given to all other classmates.

Comparing these two scores for each student, we found that jigsaw students *did* grow to like their groupmates more than they liked their other classmates, even though at the beginning they had liked their groupmates slightly *less* than their other classmates. Moreover, this increased liking for groupmates did not occur at the expense of the others, because liking for others also increased, although it did not increase nearly as much as the liking for groupmates. In short, *by the end of the study, the students liked both groupmates and other classmates better than when the study began.* Thus jigsaw has a generally favorable effect on the liking of students for each other throughout the class—especially within each working group.

THE ATTITUDE QUESTIONNAIRE

The second instrument, the attitude questionnaire, allowed us to determine the differences in attitudes between students in the jigsaw classes and students in the control classes. The attitudes covered such dimensions as liking for school, self-esteem, and competitiveness. For each dimension we compared the answers given by students in the jigsaw classes with the answers given by students in the control classes. The results follow.

Liking for School

Casual observation suggests that in traditional teacher-oriented classrooms, boredom grows as time goes on. As boredom grows, dissatisfaction grows. What happens in jigsaw classrooms? To test this hypothesis, we combined the answers to these questions:

How much do you like school this year?
When you are in the classroom, how happy do you feel?
When you are in the classroom, how bored do you feel?

At the end of six weeks, students in the control classes liked school less than they had at the beginning. Students in the jigsaw classes, however, liked school as well as they had at the beginning. This confirmed our hypothesis: jigsaw groups do help students sustain interest in school, thus combating the declining interest that we found in teacher-oriented classes.

Since students in the study were from several ethnic groups, it is reasonable to assume that they might have had somewhat different answers to the same questions. For that reason, we looked at each ethnic group separately. In fact, whites, African-American, and Latinos did differ in their answers to the questions about liking school. Whites in the jigsaw groups grew to like school more during the six weeks while whites in the control classes liked school less. So, for whites, the jigsaw groups actually caused an increase in liking for school. In contrast, the African-American students in the jigsaw groups liked school slightly less, but they still liked school more than the African-Americans in the control classes did. Thus, for African-American students, the jigsaw groups succeeded in reducing a tendency to lose interest in school. Results for the Latino students were quite different and surprising. Those in the control classes showed an increase in liking for school that was greater than the increase in liking for school in the jigsaw classes.

To what can we attribute this unexpected finding for the Latino students? One possible explanation is traceable to the language problems encountered by Latino students. In traditional classrooms, they often learn how to keep quiet, and the longer they are in the classroom the more comfortable they may become with this state of affairs. Along comes the jigsaw technique, which forces them to undergo the discomfort of speaking English, a situation that may cause them to like school less during the initial six-week testing period. If this speculation is true, we would expect their liking for school to increase after prolonged exposure to the jigsaw—that is, after they become accustomed to speaking more in school. Or, in a similar vein, if Latino students were in a situation where they would not feel embarrassed by any difficulty with language—for example, if they were in the majority in the classroom—they would not be susceptible to discomfort in the jigsaw situation.

To test this, Robert Geffner, one of the students assisting us at the time, conducted the same experiment in classrooms in Watsonville, California, where Latinos are in the majority. In general Geffner replicated our findings, and in addition showed that, in this situation, Latino children tended to like school better in the jigsaw situation than in competitive classrooms.

Overall, students in the jigsaw classes grew to like school more than students in control classes. We also learned of these positive effects in other, more casual ways. Both students and teachers involved in the jigsaw groups informally commented on the fun that students had in the groups. They enjoyed the freedom to "behave," to interact with their classmates, and to move around more freely than in a traditional classroom. In addition, the students expressed satisfaction with their involvement in their own learning, which was an important part of the group experience.

Self-Esteem

For all of us, the term *self-concept* can generally be defined as the attitudes, abilities, and assumptions that we hold concerning ourselves and that act as a guide for behavior. The evaluative component of our self-concept is *self-esteem,* the degree of worth and power that we perceive in ourselves. Where do we each find evidence about our own worth and power? A major source of self-worth and power is the result of interpersonal interactions with relevant others, such as family members, teachers, and friends. David Franks and Joseph Marolla have termed this *outer self-esteem.* Another source of self-esteem *(inner self-esteem)* is a function of real accomplishment: success or failure in a person's interaction with the environment. Both factors can be enormously important in the classroom.

In education, these two dimensions of sell-esteem develop from a child's interpretation of the feedback from teachers and classmates as well as from individual learning experiences. According to attribution theory, which has been tested by researchers such as Fritz Heider and E. E. Jones, individuals have a tendency to go beyond the available information in order to try to explain the causes of someone's behavior—even their own. In general, when viewing their own behavior, individuals will explain their successes by personal attributions (i.e., "Success was due to my ability"), and resort to situational attributions in trying to explain failure (i.e., "My failure was due to feeling sick that day"). Thus self-attributions generally protect self-esteem. In the classroom, then, a student would probably attribute a good performance to personal ability, knowledge, intelligence, etc., which would enhance inner self-esteem. Indeed, M. V. Covington and Richard Beery report that success-oriented students generally make personal attributions when they perform well and usually attribute failure to a lack of effort. In addition, there is substantial evidence that students with high self-esteem generally have high achievement levels in school. In summaries of the research in this field, it has been suggested that high self-esteem leads to better achievement and, conversely, that high performance leads to a high self-esteem. It appears that positive experiences, personal attributions, higher expectations, and anticipated success are all involved in self-fulfilling prophecies that lead to improved self-esteem and subsequently to higher achievement levels in school.

What happens when a child experiences failure? Research results reported by Covington and Beery indicate that the lack of successful experiences and the scarcity of rewards in the classroom can lead some students to learn to expect failure. These students give up and stop trying to succeed: low self-esteem and low achievement are maintained through negative self-fulfilling prophecies. In these cases it appears that the students make situational attributions (e.g., luck) for the few successes they might have, and personal attributions for their failures (e.g., poor ability and low self-worth). These same types of attributions are often made by classmates and even by some teachers with regard to those students who are failing in school. Thus the interactions among students can also lead to these self-defeating and self-fulfilling prophecies. Clearly, competitiveness exacerbates this process.

It is sometimes assumed that working cooperatively blunts individuality and therefore makes people feel less important as individuals. Just as we did not want to enhance student liking by creating cohesive but antagonistic teams, neither did we want to foster group interdependence at the expense of individual feelings of self-esteem. It is our contention that the reverse happens: that people who work together receive encouragement and positive feedback from their coworkers more often than not—because of the interdependence of the situation. Moreover, in the process of working together individuals learn to trust their own effectiveness. The combination of these two processes should lead to an increase in self-esteem. We felt that this would be particularly true in our situation because of the fact that individual performance on a test is a child's own. That is, while children *learn* cooperatively, their scores on exams are a reflection of each individual's mastery of the material, not an average of the group score.

This hypothesis was tested by combining the results of three questions:

How much do you like being yourself?
When you are in the classroom, how important do you feel?
When you are in class, how often do you feel you can learn whatever you try to learn?

As before, the answers given by students in jigsaw classes were compared to the answers of students in control classes.

As suspected, this comparison showed that during the six-week period *students in the jigsaw classes increased in self-esteem to a greater extent than students in competitive classes.* Apparently, giving students the opportunity to participate in teaching as well as in learning made them feel like they were an important part of the learning process, and thus that they were worthy individuals. In competitive classrooms, such as our control classes, students were primarily recipients rather than givers of information, a situation that apparently did little to involve students actively in the learning process or to enhance their positive feelings about themselves. As the story told by one of the teachers earlier in this chapter indicates, Paul was no longer seen as dumb by his classmates. Being valued by his peers was an important step toward higher self-esteem.

Competition

Does the jigsaw experience change students' attitudes toward competing and winning at all costs? It was hypothesized that compared to students in the competitive classes, students in the jigsaw classes would have a decreased preference for competitive behaviors. This hypothesis was tested by the questionnaire item, "I would rather beat a classmate than help him." The answers indicate that students in the jigsaw classes grew less competitive over the six weeks while students in the control classes grew more competitive.

This lowered competitiveness seemed to extend beyond the classroom groups as well. As mentioned at the beginning of this chapter, jigsaw teachers reported that teachers not involved in our study but teaching the students at some time each week (e.g., music or physical education teachers) remarked about the improved attitudes and behavior of the jigsaw students. It seems that classroom exposure to cooperation produced a lessening of unproductive competitiveness in related settings as well as in the classroom.

Learning from Others

Another important aspect of our results concerns students' views about whether or not they felt other students could be a source of learning for them. The question "Can you learn anything from other kids in your class?" was the test of this hypothesis. We found that over the six weeks students in the jigsaw classes increasingly believed they could learn from other students. Conversely, students in the control classes decreased in this belief. The experience of teaching and being taught by classmates was clearly a successful one for the students in the jigsaw groups: They did learn to use their peers as resources. The results of this hypothesis provide an exciting kind of support for our enthusiasm about the jigsaw groups: The students who participate in this method of teaching report that it works.

ACADEMIC PERFORMANCE IN THE JIGSAW CLASSROOM

Although we have shown that jigsaw groups provide many benefits for students, we have presented no data on the academic performance of students in more typical classrooms. No matter how much happiness and self-confidence a teaching technique provides, it is of dubious benefit to students if" it interferes with their mastery of the subject matter. Previous and subsequent research conducted by other investigators suggests that academic performance would be *at least as high* with the jigsaw as it is with more typical classroom techniques. For example, research shows that both pupils and tutors achieve academic gains following peer tutoring.

In order to investigate this question, we conducted a separate study to measure the effects of the jigsaw technique on academic performance. Our study lasted two weeks and involved about 300 fifth- and sixth-grade students from five elementary schools in Austin. Six jigsaw teachers and five teachers using competitive classroom approaches participated in the study. The latter teachers were highly competent and respected; their classes had approximately the same ethnic composition and reading skills as the jigsaw classes. The curriculum consisted of a unit on colonial America taken from a fifth-grade textbook, plus supplementary materials. For the jigsaw classes, the curriculum content was partitioned for jigsaw presentation, but otherwise it was identical to that used in the competitive classes.

Before the unit was introduced, a pretest was given on the materials on colonial America. After the unit was completed, a posttest was administered. The data showed that before the unit was begun there was no difference in knowledge about colonial America between students in jigsaw and competitive classes. However, after the unit was completed, students in the jigsaw groups scored considerably higher on the posttest than did students in competitive classes. Looking at the test scores by ethnic groups, it was clear that *the difference in performance between jigsaw and competitive classes was primarily due to the scores of the minority students.* Specifically, these data suggested that in integrated schools whites learned equally well in both jigsaw and competitive classes, but African-Americans and Latinos learned *much more* in jigsaw than in competitive classes.

JIGSAW AND THE FORMATION OF EMPATHY FOR OTHERS

Why does the jigsaw strategy produce such positive results? A recent experiment by Samuel Gaertner and his colleagues demonstrates that what seems to happen is that the process of cooperation lowers barriers between people from various ethnic and racial groups by changing the cognitive categories people use. In other words, cooperation changes our tendency to categorize the outgroup from "those people" to "us." In addition, the jigsaw technique encourages the development of empathy—the ability to put oneself in another person's shoes. It should be clear that anything that increases a persons empathy is beneficial to human relations, enhancing helping behavior and decreasing aggression. In the classroom, the best way to maximize learning—especially in the jigsaw situation—is to pay close attention to the child who is speaking. For example, if I am in a jigsaw group with Carlos and want to learn what he knows, not only must I listen attentively to him but I must also put myself in his shoes in order to be able to ask him useful questions—questions that are clearly stated and that are nonthreatening to him. In the process, I learn a lot not only about the subject matter and about Carlos but about the process of seeing the world through another person's eyes.

This was brilliantly demonstrated in 1981 in an experiment conducted by Diane Bridgeman, one of our graduate students. Bridgeman administered a sequence of cartoons to ten-year-old children, half of whom had spent eight weeks participating in jigsaw classes. The cartoons were aimed at measuring a child's ability to empathize. In one cartoon, for example, a little boy looks sad as he says good-bye to his father at the airport. In the next frame, a letter carrier delivers a package to the child. When the boy opens it, he finds a toy airplane—and promptly bursts into tears. When Bridgeman asked the children why the little boy cried, almost all of the children told her the reason: The airplane reminded the child of being separated from his father, which made him sad.

So far so good. Now for the crucial part. Bridgeman asked the children what the letter carrier who delivered the package was thinking. Most children that age make a consistent error, based on the egocentric assumption that their own knowledge is universal; specifically, they erroneously assume *the letter carrier* would know the boy was sad because the gift reminded him of his father leaving. The responses of the children who had participated in the jigsaw classes followed a different pattern, however. Because of their jigsaw experience, they were better able to take the letter carrier's perspective; they knew he was not privy to the same information they were and that he wasn't aware of the scene at the airport. Accordingly, the jigsaw children realized the letter carrier would experience *confusion* at the sight of a little boy crying over receiving a nice present. In sum, participation in jigsaw groups has a general impact on a child's ability' to see the world through another person's eyes; this seems to be a major cause of the beneficial effects described above—and is a key to the reduction of prejudice and the creation of caring and constructive interpersonal relations.

CHAPTER 8

SHARING JIGSAW: AN IN-SERVICE WORKSHOP

If you want to use—and master—the jigsaw technique in your classroom we recommend that you do more than read about it. It would be most useful to experience what it is like to work effectively in small groups in order to enrich your understanding of the underlying theory that contributed to the development of jigsaw and in order to have a firsthand understanding of what your students will be experiencing. In this chapter, we will describe an in-service workshop designed primarily to help teachers learn to use the jigsaw technique. This chapter can also be looked upon as a guidebook for in-service workshops—a vehicle for training others so that little or no outside consultation will be necessary.

The basic jigsaw skills can be learned in one day. However, we should point out that, in an ideal world, five days of training would be best, allowing a leisurely time frame that will enable teachers to reach the point where they can move easily into the jigsaw method with a great deal of facility, skill, and confidence. The added time would be extremely useful in providing teachers the opportunity to develop materials for classroom use in consultation with one another. However, we fully understand the real world—which means that most in-service workshops are one-day affairs, and so the objectives must be limited. Nevertheless, a great deal can be learned in one day.

There are several background considerations that will contribute to the success of any workshop—and to the subsequent success of the jigsaw method in the classroom:

1. Participants should attend a workshop voluntarily. In our experience, unless the motivation comes from within, there is likely to be resistance and resentment.

2. If possible, participants should attend the workshop as a part of a school team. This will provide some on-site support once the workshop is over.

3. Time should be set aside during the workshop to develop the special learning materials required by the jigsaw method. If teachers can work

together to develop these materials during the workshop, less individual time will be required of the teacher later.

4. Workshop staff should follow up and support participants once they are back in the classroom.

OBJECTIVES

In the jigsaw workshop, teachers learn about cooperation primarily by *experiencing* cooperation. The workshop has a flow to it that parallels the development of cooperative group work in the classroom. It can be divided into three distinct sections:

1. During an initial period, individual participants begin to be transformed into a cooperative working group. This is a time for them to get to know one another, to discover their own reasons for attending the workshop, to be able to present themselves and their skills to one another and to begin to get acquainted with the range of resources others have brought to the group.
2. Participants are immersed in a series of structured exercises designed to develop group cohesiveness. The usefulness of these techniques in the classroom is discussed along with issues related to team-building activities in general. These activities allow participants the opportunity to interact and to develop resources among their colleagues as well as to provide a structure for the participants to share ideas and give each other support. This common understanding and support system can be of great significance for the teachers after they return to the classroom.
3. The *content* of the workshop—cooperative education in general and jigsaw in particular—is introduced partly in a lecture format and ultimately through the jigsaw technique itself so that the content and the process dovetails.

Accomplishing all of these objectives in a one-day workshop requires a full schedule of carefully planned activities. We present here one of several possible workshop designs—one that we have found particularly successful. Under each time slot are listed directions for that segment of the workshop followed by a rationale for those directions. Readers who have conducted in-service workshops and have developed a style that suits them individually may wish to adapt some of the instructions to their own style, or they may even wish to simply skim this chapter. Individuals who are new to this kind of activity or who have suffered through in-service workshops without knowing why they were structured the way they were may want to read this chapter more care-fully, particularly the sections explaining the rationale for team-building ex-ercises.

INSTRUCTIONS AND RATIONALE

8:30-8:45   (15 minutes)
1.   Coffee and time for informal discussion
The leader, or facilitator, announces that the workshop will begin at 8:45; the leader should keep track of how many participants have not yet arrived.
Rationale
Providing a rough idea of the schedule helps the participants feel more com-fortable by letting them know what to expect. As in any learning situation, it is important to give time limits so that participants can pace themselves.

8:45-9:00   (15 minutes)
2.   Brief lecture
The facilitator focuses on the need for developing cooperation in the class-room and describes the day's schedule. The subject matter discussed in this minilecture is flexible. Topics might include difficulties encountered in a com-petitive society; problems at-risk students and students from other cultures may face in the classroom and how these problems may be related to compet-itive classroom environment; and how cooperative strategies might help solve these problems. Material from the first chapter of this book could be useful.

Rationale
The minilecture is given early, even though participants are rarely settled enough to listen carefully. It is given informally without a prepared text in order to create a relaxed atmosphere. Delivering information in the traditional classroom manner allows participants to ease into the topic of the day and provides them with a cognitive framework that will help them understand what follows and why they are being encouraged to participate.

9:00-9:20   (20 minutes)
3.   Transition: Team-building activity/icebreaker
The facilitator explains the exercise: "As you know, before any group activity in the classroom can work, the teacher needs to prepare students in such a way that they are ready to work together. In a little while, we are going to be discussing techniques that you've found effective in your teaching, but first we need to engage in some team-building activities so that when we get into discussion groups we will all be able to work effectively. We want you to ex-

perience these activities, to see if you might use them in your classroom. First, we need to get better acquainted with the resources we have here. The first activity will help us begin to know each other."

If the number of participants is less than 15, ask each person, beginning with the workshop leader, to give his name, a brief description of his professional background and interest, and a summary of what he hopes to learn during the day.

With a larger group of teachers (15 to 20) give participants newsprint and felt markers and ask them to draw a picture or write something that will represent them in two ways: (1) professional life and (2) personal interests. Ask participants to do this nonverbally and to take only five minutes to complete their "advertisements" of who they are. Then ask them to put their names somewhere prominently on the newsprint and, without talking, to walk around holding the newsprint in front of them and read other people's advertisements while others read theirs.

If the silence is too uncomfortable, inform the participants that they may ask each other a few questions as they mill in a circle. They should try to remember some people who share their interests or who would be interesting to talk with, and they should then find one person they don't know well, sit down together, and introduce themselves.

Rationale

Once participants begin to get to know each other, to get comfortable, and feel accepted in the larger group, their energies can be directed toward the content at hand. Most people feel some discomfort, anxiety, or even irritation at the beginning of a workshop. If this is not attended to early, participants may become restless and resistant to the activities. Helping participants move past these initial feelings may require making them even more uncomfortable temporarily, but once the ice has been broken, a relaxed, cooperative atmosphere can be established.

Resistance to a structured ice-breaking activity can be handled by discussing parallels to teaching situations in the classroom. Teachers are often faced with situations in which it is hard to induce a positive outlook in students toward some activity they know the students will enjoy and learn from in the long run.

9:20-9:40 (20 minutes)
4. Working in pairs

Directions along the following lines can now be given: "In order to establish a cooperative classroom atmosphere at the beginning of the year, it is important that the students get to know each other. One useful technique is to have them pair up to interview each other in a special way. We are going try that exercise in just a moment. Not only will it give us an inside view of what we can do with our own students, it will be helpful in facilitating our own acquaintance process right here in this room. What I would like each of you to do is to think of three questions that would help you get to know your partner better. The temptation may be simply to ask your partner questions like 'Where do you live?' and 'Do you know so and so?' Then both of you might continue discussing in a more or less superficial way that person whom you both happen to know. What I would like for us to do is think of three questions that will really help us get to know our partners better. Here are some effective questions you might ask: 'Think of a close friend of yours; if you were to ask that person what she wishes you would change about yourself, what might she say?' 'When were you happiest in the last month?' 'What has irritated you most in the last week?' Or you might want to think up questions of your own. Please take a minute silently too think of any three questions which will help you to get to know your partner better."

The next exercise will demonstrate the process of active listening. The following directions are given: "We will also make this interviewing process into a listening exercise. In order to learn effective communication, your students will have to practice effective listening. This is a technique that can be taught to even very young children. Practicing the 'active' part of active listening requires that the listener summarize the essence of the speaker's comments until the speaker says, 'Yes, you understand what I have said.' Then proceed to the next question. For example, after your partner has answered a question, rephrase it, trying to get to the meaning of what was said by expanding it a little or clarifying it. When your partner indicates that, yes, you have understood her, go on to ask a new question. You will need to listen closely to your partner and to remember what she says because you will be tested on it. That is, in a few minutes you will be asked to introduce your partner to another two couples by sharing what you have learned about her. You will have about five minutes for this."

Rationale

Most of the rationale here is contained within the directions. The more the leader can share the rationale behind what she is doing, the more willing and able the participants are to follow the directions. Teachers know their students need to develop their listening skills.

The directions for this exercise might seem unnecessarily long. However, it is probably better to give the directions all at once, rather than to try to interrupt the group, wait for them to be silent, and give them more directions. With a large group it is difficult to get everyone to stop talking at the same time.

By providing participants with a specific number of questions to ask, there is less likelihood that they will wander off the subject. With students, asking them to write down their questions greatly increases the likelihood that the questions will be carefully composed.

When a leader is moving large groups of people from one activity to another, it is very important to give them a one- or two-minute warning, announced loudly while participants are still talking. The information about the time remaining will give them a chance to end their discussion.

9:40-9:55   (15 minutes)
5. Pairs working with pairs

The instructions for this transition are as follows: "We are going to take a break in fifteen minutes. Before we do that, I'd like to ask each pair to join two other pairs to form a six-person group. Try to join with people you don't know very well. Then introduce your partner, providing some information you learned about her."

After seven or eight minutes, when the groups seem to be finished with their introductions, the leader explains how this can be transferred to the classroom: "We had you join the six-person group, with a partner as a support base. In the classroom, before having discussion groups introduce a topic, it is useful to have students first write down two ideas about the topic, and then share those ideas with one other person. This strategy is found in many cooperative learning methods and even young children can practice consulting a neighbor to arrive at an answer. With this experience, they come to more complex group work with some skills already well developed. Writing down the ideas gives students something specific to say, and rehearsing the expression of those ideas with a partner helps make it easier for them to participate in the groups. It is easier first to make contact with just one person, and then, with that person, to join four strangers." The leader now asks participants to discuss what they gave up in order to be here today, and what they hope to gain from the workshop.

Rationale

The session has been going for almost an hour, and the participants will be wanting a break. For design purposes, the break fits better in a few minutes; so to avoid distraction it is important to let the group know they can anticipate a break soon.

The leader should interrupt gently but firmly. There may be one or two groups that haven't quite finished, just as there may be some that finished early and are beginning to get bored. The leader must sense the proper time to intervene, even at the expense of cutting off or postponing a discussion: "If you are not quite finished, you may want to continue during the break."

Five or ten minutes of discussion on two final topics, ambivalence and purpose, can save a lot of time later. At the beginning of a workshop, participants may devote much energy to wishing they were doing something else. This creates a resistance to focusing on what is happening. The mere sharing of their ambivalence helps them move past their resistance, and allows them to then enter into a positive discussion of what their goals for the workshop are. The clearer they are about their objectives, the more likely it is these objectives will be met.

9:55-10:20 (20-25 minutes)
6. Break
The leader asks participants to remember what group they are in, and then announces a break of from 10 to 20 minutes, depending upon how tight the schedule is. *Rationale*

Although times are stated with precision, flexibility is usually warranted. Consequently, most workshops usually run at least ten minutes behind schedule at this point, so the break may not run as long as is indicated here.

SUMMARY

Let's reflect on what has been accomplished during this past hour:

- Participants have briefly discussed the need for cooperation in the classroom.
- They have become acquainted with the resources in the room and other participants. During the break, they will be able to approach people that they think they might want to know better.
- They have had the opportunity to develop a support base with one other person, a partner with whom they can more effectively enter a six-person group.
- They have had a chance to express their possible ambivalence about attending the workshop and to focus on what they hope to get out of it.
- The leader has shown how the exercises might be used in the classroom and has sensitized the participants to several issues related to leading team-building activities.

Now let's return to the workshop.

10:20-11:30   (70 minutes)
7. Group Process Exercise: Fish-bowling
About three minutes before the end of the break, the leader announces that the fish-bowling session will begin in a few minutes. Participants should return to their six-person groups and chat for a few minutes.

FISH-BOWLING

The leader introduces this exercise by reminding participants of the importance of understanding the dynamics of any group that must work together. This is particularly true for students in the classroom. The leader points out that it is necessary for students to develop the skills needed to change their group process in such a way as to make it more productive and rewarding. *Fish-bowling* is a useful activity that can be used to develop these skills. One group sits in a circle and talks about some topic while another group sits on the outside and watches very carefully what is going on inside the group. Later the observers become the observed.

The leader begins by suggesting two topics for discussion: "What type of students seem to gain from competitive environments" and "When competitive strategies in the classroom help increase learning." While the first group is discussing that topic, the second group should be observing that group on four criteria, which should be explained and then displayed prominently in the room:

Observing Group Process

1. **What is the energy level of the group?** Are people sitting up or slouching? Do they appear interested or are they seemingly withdrawn from discussion? What might be reasons for disinterest or active participation?
2. **Does leadership emerge in the group?** Who starts the group moving on a particular topic? Can one person in the group easily be called the leader? Does the leader help facilitate the group's discussion by summarizing what has been said so discussion may proceed? Does one member help the group stick to the topic and not wander off? Does that person help the group move along when it has reached consensus?
3. **Is there a climate of listening?** Are people making eye contact with one another? Are they nodding to indicate they understand what has been said? Are they rephrasing and summarizing what other people have said, indicating active listening?
4. **Does everyone participate in the group?** Are all members invited to share their ideas, or do they have to interrupt the discussion to say something? Does every member participate, or do some members sit silently? (If some members do not want to participate that is OK, as long as they know they are welcome to join in.)

In addition to these criteria observers can pay attention to any other aspect of the group process they deem important. They should make notes on what processes they observe because they too will be getting into the center and discussing their group process.

After 10 minutes, the groups change places. When discussing the process, the leader should remind participants to be as constructive as possible by focusing on specific behaviors and what they think the effects of those behaviors were. This should be done in a nonjudgmental way

After five minutes, participants should note their emotional reactions. Some may be feeling defensive even if they were saying mostly positive things about the group. The inside group may be temporarily more cohesive because it is having to face outside evaluation. If this is done in a classroom, it may be best to limit the critiquing to no more than two minutes at the beginning. During such a brief interval, most of the comments will be quite positive. Moreover, the early positive effects, or early learnings, of fish-bowling are not from the critiques as much as from the attempts of the group on the inside to be an effective team because it is being observed by another group. Participants may be aware of how much better their group behavior is when another group is observing them. While this situation may seem forced after a few days group members will behave more spontaneously while still trying to make their group an effective one. Later, when the groups have a higher level of trust and when they have the skills to communicate the feedback in a way that is constructive, the critiquing can be extended to five or ten minutes.

At the end of this, the group leader summarizes what has been learned and which group dynamics made groups go well and which ones hindered them. Participants can be asked how they experienced the exercise and how it might be used in the classroom.

Rationale

Most of the rationale for this exercise is given within the directions. The participants are learning on three levels:

1. They are learning by experiencing (as participants) the *process* of the various exercises. They will now empathize better when their students participate in similar activities.
2. They are learning from each other the *content* of the topics. The particular topic chosen is not crucial. It must merely be of interest, and one that relates to effective teaching. For our purposes we chose the topic of competition, a useful motivator that may also have detrimental effects.
3. They are learning as they watch the leader model and explain *effective behavior.*

11:30-11:45 (15 minutes)
Question-and-answer period

11:45-1:30 (1 hour 45 minutes)
Lunch.

1:30-1:40   (10 minutes)
8. Reassemble
Participants return to their six-person groups and discuss any issues raised earlier. *Rationale*

This time allows participants to share any thoughts and opinions they might have had over lunch, and to get settled into their groups and get ready to work on the next task.

EXPERIENCING JIGSAW

9.

The next step provides participants with a jigsaw experience—the most important part of the workshop. It is the time that participants first immerse themselves in the actual jigsaw process. The topic will be jigsaw. Thus they will simultaneously learn about the jigsaw process by experiencing it, by listening to others, and by discussing it. Through active involvement, the participants are able to absorb the necessary information more easily and efficiently.

A packet of workshop materials is given to one person in each group, who will be designated the leader for this exercise. (These materials consist of six cards, each one containing a one-paragraph description of a basic point in the jigsaw process. Each group member receives one card. The group leader explains the next step: "You each have a paragraph covering some issue associated with the use of the jigsaw technique. Study your paragraph for five minutes and think about how you can best teach the group about that issue. For example, if your card is about the importance of team-building, try to prepare for leading a discussion on that topic, by reading through the paragraph, seeing what the ideas are, and then relating them to your own classroom experiences."

During the five-minute planning time, participants should jot down some of the ways they can elicit group discussion on their topic. For instance, they may want to begin their section with a fantasy about the beginning of the school year: how the kids are going to be feeling about each other and how getting to know each other will be important. Or they may want to begin with a brief role-playing of a disruptive, ineffective group. Or they may merely want to begin with asking questions about what teambuilding exercises might be useful at the beginning of the year. The goal is to draw the members into a discussion during which they teach each other about the importance of team-building.

At the end of the planning time, each participant will take a turn leading a five-minute discussion on his or her particular topic.

Rationale

Since all participants will in turn be responsible for teaching some topic, as group members they will tend to be supportive of the topic leaders, and will try to make discussion productive.

1:50-2:25   (35 minutes)

10.   Teaching

The group leader should designate a timekeeper, since the group as a whole will have only 30 minutes to cover all six topics, and remind participants that each will have only five minutes. Then the person with the first paragraph should begin.

While the groups are working, the workshop facilitator moves around answering questions and observing the dynamics of each group. She should make comments about group process to the leader of the group, suggesting, for example, that the group should move on to the next topic. At the beginning, if members are still preparing their topic rather than listening to the discussion, it should be pointed out. If the participants are talking to the topic leader, they should be encouraged to talk to the group as a whole.

Rationale

The group timekeeper wall help the group focus on its task and keep the discussion progressing. Here is the opportunity for the facilitator to point out the importance of time limits in increasing group productivity.

This exercise will enable participants to help each other do the best job of teaching they can, and also to increase interest in the topic. It should become apparent to them that they already know much of the information necessary to use jigsaw. They might also discover that as a group they have many resources for helping each other learn to be effective facilitators in their classrooms.

Initially, groups need assistance in becoming productive. This assistance should come primarily from within the group; hence the facilitator works through the leaders to validate their authority, instead of giving direct assistance.

2:25-2:45   (20 minutes)

11.   Group process evaluation and break

As each group finishes, the leader announces that there will be a break after all participants write down five things they noticed about the group process. They can refer to the process questions which were used for the fish-bowl exercise in the morning. Participants should spend about five minutes working quietly, and then take a 15-minute break.

Rationale

Since there will be a break, it is not essential that all the groups finish at the same time. However, the facilitator should not let participants work more than five minutes into their break, because they will need at least a 10-minute break in order to keep working effectively. The reasons for having participants write their observations about group process are twofold. First, it will help them to remember their ideas for a discussion after the break. Second, it increases the likelihood that these thoughts will be verbalized in discussion.

2:45-2:55   (10 minutes)
12.   Fish-Bowling

Participants return to their groups and the facilitator gives directions along the following lines: "In a moment you will have five minutes to discuss how your group worked together in the jigsaw exercise. I'd like you to do this by telling the others what you liked about what they did, and what you thought they could do better. If you wish, refer to your notes but try not to merely read them to the others. This will help keep the discussion flowing spontaneously.

"So you can also learn how the other groups functioned, we are going to fish-bowl this discussion. This will encourage the group on the inside to critique itself thoroughly and also to attend to its present group process. The group on the outside will again take notes on the process of the other group, using the criteria posted this morning. Members of the outside group will then move to the center and will have five minutes to give their observations."

Rationale

Again, the rationale here is contained within the directions. One additional reason for a fish-bowl is to give participants more experience in observing group processes.

In the directions, we usually tell them (1) what they are going to do; (2) why they are going to do it; and (3) what to begin doing. Even though 1 and 3 are the same, participants often miss the directions and require a third or fourth repetition.

13.   Fish-bowling: Reverse Groups

Have the groups switch seats, with the members of the outside group moving inside and discussing for five minutes what they observed about the first group's process. The new outside group will begin taking notes on the new inside group's process.

3:00-3:05 (5 minutes)

14.

The inside group discusses its own process during the jig-saw exercise. Group members may refer to the notes taken, if necessary. The outside group will continue to write down observations of the inside group's process.

3:05-3:10 (5 minutes)

15.

The groups switch seats again, with the outside group members moving inside and discussing for five minutes what they observed about the other groups process.

3:10-3:50 (40 minutes)

16. Discussion

All participants form one large group, and discuss how to implement the jigsaw technique drawing on both the information and the experiences they have had that day. The participants will probably want to share descriptions of effective team-building exercises and will want to discuss problem situations.

Rationale

Many questions and suggestions will have been stimulated by the day's activities. This discussion gives them time to put everything together. We often discuss specifically what has been working in jigsaw classrooms.

3:50-4:00 (10 minutes)

17. Evaluation

Each participant is given an evaluation sheet on which to give feedback for improving the workshop.

Rationale

It is important for workshop facilitators, as well as for classroom teachers, to invite feedback regularly. Not only is the feedback useful to the facilitator or teacher but, by increasing the participant or student's sense of ownership and control, it quickens interest and builds morale.

This workshop was originally scheduled to end at 4:30. We usually end our workshops 30 minutes early in order to give teachers a needed rest. Also, this encourages them to give their complete attention to the end of the workshop.

If there is more time another day, this design could be readily expanded by including such exercises as the Broken Squares game (described in Chapter 3). Even more important, teachers could work on adapting their curriculum for use with jigsaw. Another useful task is for the participants to take a few minutes to form three- or four-person "support groups." If participants have not come to the workshop in school teams, then these groups can meet periodically so teachers can share ideas and develop curriculum material. Ideally, each group would consist of same-grade-level teachers whose schools are near one another.

One of the purposes of this one-day workshop is to whet teachers' appetites for more. Even with a great deal of support, it has been our experience that teachers can benefit greatly from further training and from sharing experiences. After even one brief workshop, however, they should be able to implement some jigsaw strategies in their classrooms.

CHAPTER 9

COOPERATION IN THE CONTEXT
OF A COMPETITIVE SOCIETY

Picture the following scene: Two ten-year-old boys are facing each other across a table, playing a game. In each boy's hand is a string connected to a plastic block which holds a small round marble in a hole. The marble holder can be moved in either direction, depending on which string is pulled. At first glance, the activity bears a superficial resemblance to a game of tug-of-war, with the object being to pull the plastic holder toward oneself so that the marble will drop into a goal on either end of the table. But, as the boys soon learn, the game differs from tug-of-war in one crucial way: the marble holder is constructed in such a way that if both players pull hard (as in tug-of-war), it will break apart—and neither player will succeed in pulling the marble to his goal. In short, the boys are not playing a competitive game; in order for one child to achieve his goal, the other child needs to relax his string. Each child has been informed that for each marble he succeeds in pulling to his goal, he will receive a prize. Clearly, the sensible strategy will be some form of turn taking. In that way, each child will attain a prize in 50 percent of the trials.

This game is an example of the kind of game-playing situation utilized in a series of provocative experiments, performed in the 1960s and 1970s by Spencer Kagan and his colleagues. How do children perform in this kind of game? Well, to a large extent it depends on the early family/cultural experiences of the individual child. It turns out that most white, Anglo-Saxon children perform rather poorly on this task. In this and similar games, they tend to behave in "irrationally competitive" ways—for example, pulling hard and breaking the marble holder apart on trial after trial— so that neither player ends up with many prizes. In this kind of game the behavior of most Anglo-Saxon children stands in sharp contrast to Latinos and African-Americans as well as Israelis raised on kibbutz (but not those raised in cities) who, for the most part, have little or no difficulty in developing a cooperative, turn-taking mode of playing. These results indicate either that, with very few exceptions, white American children have not mastered the skill of cooperation or that they fail to recognize a situation where a cooperative strategy would be in their own best interest. Either way, they seem to have a severely limited perspective and are stuck with a narrow range of coping skills.

COOPERATION: PRAGMATICS—NOT IDEOLOGY

In our zeal to convince the readers of this book that cooperation is a good thing, we are aware that occasionally we get carried away and may be giving the false impression that we are opposed to competition. The truth is, we *do* believe in competition—and that it can be fun. For example, we love to play sports—like tennis and basketball—and when we play these games we try hard to win and are fully aware of the fact that they would be less fun if we didn't keep score; that is, the competitive aspect of these games adds zest and fun to the endeavor. What we are opposed to is not competition per se; it is *relentless,* unmitigated competition, where, in the words of the great football coach, Vince Lombardi, "winning isn't everything, it's the *only* thing!" We believe that competition can be exhilarating, but there are other things in life that can be just as exhilarating. And one of those things is cooperation. Cooperation is not only joyous, but in an increasingly complex world, where very few important things can be accomplished by a single individual, *the ability to cooperate is a skill that must be mastered for survival.*

In most endeavors in our society, competition is so pervasive, it leaves no room for the learning of cooperative skills. Here's an example of what we are talking about. We frequently give speeches to parent-teacher organizations in which we describe the benefits of jigsaw. Occasionally during the question-and-answer period, we have received comments from concerned parents that take the following form:

> "This is all well and good; but how is my 10-year-old daughter ever going to get into medical school if she spends her life learning cooperation while other children are learning how to compete? Won't that put her at a serious disadvantage?"

The question is a fair and reasonable one—cutting right to the heart of the problem. If our society is largely competitive, does training children to cooperate too much diminish their ability[7] to win in such competitive situations as gaining admittance to college or medical school—as well as succeeding in the allegedly cutthroat world of business? In short, are we grooming our children for failure? Such questions make us wonder if in our speeches we have been doing a good enough job of presenting the case for jigsaw. For, in our minds, in this culture, parents being worried that their children might not be exposed to sufficient competition (because of participating in the jigsaw class-room), is akin to a person who tips the scales at 350 pounds worrying that using an artificial sweetener in his coffee might cause him to lose too much weight! In other words in our society, we are bombarded with competitiveness and children will never experience a lack of exposure to it. Most children learn to compete simply by living in our society. We believe that what children desperately need is a respite from this bombardment—an oasis, if you will, in which they can learn some other valuable skills.

Let us return to the example we used to open this chapter: In the 1960s and 1970s, white, Anglo-Saxon children were having a great deal of difficulty co-operating—even when it was clearly in their self-interest. In the 1990s a growing number of students in American classrooms understand the meaning of cooperation because they have family and ethnic backgrounds that place a great deal of value on the concept. If we systematically exclude this kind of activity from the classroom, we are unwittingly placing these children at a disadvantage because they are not being allowed to actualize things that their families taught them were important. But just as important, we are robbing the white, Anglo-Saxon children of a valuable learning experience: the opportunity to learn the skill of effective cooperation and to reap the benefits to be gleaned from the cooperative experience. It should be clear, therefore, that we see cooperative learning not as an ideology but as a pragmatic skill. *The major goal of jigsaw learning is to help children learn cooperation as a skill, one to be chosen from among other skills, and to sensitize all children to situations which require that skill.*

And, as we have shown here, jigsaw works. There is no doubt that we are overly enthusiastic about the jigsaw technique. It's true. We believe that jigsaw has developed into a practical method of learning that produces great benefits at little or no cost. But the facts—and the research—bear us out: time and time again, under controlled scientific conditions, researchers have shown that the jigsaw technique is effective in promoting self-esteem, in reducing prejudice, in increasing excitement about learning—and in improving the mastery of academic material. Teachers who have tried it have been pleased not only with its impact upon their students but with the new roles and behaviors that they (the teachers) have been able to assume in the classrooms.

But we also know that cooperative learning is not the only useful way to teach. Because we believe that no single approach to classroom learning is perfect, we believe that jigsaw should not be used exclusively. Nor does it need to be. Our research has shown that the jigsaw technique produces significant beneficial effects even when it forms only a small part of the child's day in school. Indeed, strictly speaking, in our early research, we were not really comparing "cooperative classrooms" with "competitive classrooms." Rather, we were comparing competitive classrooms with competitive classrooms in which the students participated in jigsaw groups for only four or five hours per week. In other words, the so-called "jigsaw" classrooms remained mostly competitive and still the children received enormous benefits from even that small portion of cooperative learning.

These results are very encouraging. The evidence shows that jigsaw does not need to take over the entire classroom, that it can coexist with other strategies, other methods, other events, other styles of teaching— and still produce extraordinary benefits for students.

CAN WE OVERDOSE ON COOPERATION?

Is there such a thing as too much cooperation? Probably not. Casual observation of jigsaw classrooms indicates that the beneficial effects of cooperation become stronger as more time is spent in cooperative groups. Over the years, several teachers have utilized the jigsaw technique for a much larger part of each day than was the case in our formal research groups. These teachers have succeeded in adapting their curriculum material to the jigsaw technique to the point where children were spending approximately 80 percent of their class time in cooperative groups. These teachers have reported that the beneficial results were far clearer and more dramatic than when they were able to employ cooperative learning for only an hour or two a day. Although this is only anecdotal evidence, it seems safe to say that increasing the use of cooperative methods will result in increased benefits.

Nevertheless, we believe that it is most beneficial, for students as well as for teachers, if jigsaw is utilized as part of a variety of classroom strategies that include individually guided instruction *as well as some competitive activities*. This gives all students practice in all skills.

Antoine Garibaldi, an educational social psychologist, has argued that, as important as cooperation is, it might be a mistake to attempt to eliminate competition entirely from the educational process (even if it were possible). Part of Garibaldi's argument is frankly political: that disadvantaged students—especially those who are new to our society—might need to learn how to compete so that they might stand a better chance to win their way into more fulfilling, rewarding, and powerful occupations. He has further suggested that for many ethnic minorities the culture and the family may not provide the opportunity to learn to compete. Although we believe that Garibaldi might be underestimating the number of opportunities that children have to learn competitiveness, casually, just by living in a competitive society, we see nothing wrong with his argument; perhaps, in order to play it perfectly safe, some competitiveness should be present in the classroom process. We are not extremists in the cooperative movement! In the long run, it probably does not make sense to advocate the learning of the skill of cooperation at the expense of the learning of other skills—such as the skill of competing *under appropriate conditions.*

CONDITIONS FOR INTRODUCING COMPETITION

As shown here, there is no reason why cooperative and competitive techniques cannot coexist in the same classroom. Systematic research by a great many investigators, including David and Roger Johnson, Robert Slavin, and David DeVries—as well as research on jigsaw—has demonstrated that both cooperation and competition can form a part of the classroom process without undermining the benefits of cooperation. (This research is summarized in *Learning to Cooperate, Cooperating to Learn,* Slavin et al., 1985.)

Results from one early study on jigsaw conducted by Stephan, Kennedy, and Aronson indicated that competition is less likely to produce harmful effects when it is preceded by the kinds of classroom behaviors that lead to friendly relations among the students. First, some background. As you know, researchers have found that there is a pattern to the explanations people give for why things happen. Attribution theory predicts, broadly, that people attribute the cause of events to either the person involved or to the situation. Moreover, it has been demonstrated that, in general, most of us give ourselves the benefit of the doubt when trying to attribute causes of our own success or failure. That is, for successes, we tend to take personal credit ("It is because I am smart and skillful"); however, for failures, we blame external causes, something about the situation ("The sun got in my eyes," "The exam was unfair," etc.).

But, when we observe our competitors' behavior, we don't cut them any slack. In this case, we will make a personal attribution ("He's stupid," or "He doesn't know the material"). However, when competitors succeed, we will probably attribute the reason to the situation ("It was just a matter of luck"). Clearly, all of these explanations are protective of the observer's feelings of competence and help to maintain a hope for future success because personal characteristics are stable while situations change.

The experiment by Stephan, Kennedy, and Aronson was designed to explore the pattern of attributions for success given by children playing a competitive game. Results indicated that when competing against *friends,* children behaved very gently toward them. Specifically, sixth-grade students played a game that involved throwing beanbags at a target. The situation was arranged so that some students succeeded while others failed. The students were placed in either a cooperative situation or a competitive situation. What is most interesting about the results is that when the children *competed against and beat a friend* they attributed their own success to luck rather than to their own superiority, as would be predicted by attribution theory. This suggests that once friendship and empathy have been established, competition may not result in the pattern of self-centered attributions that can be demoralizing for the loser and harmful to the relationship between the winner and the loser. So, what does this mean in the classroom? Based on these research data, *competitiveness should not be introduced into the classroom situation until friendships have begun to form as a result of cooperative strategies.* This would be particularly important in classrooms today as they become increasingly diverse ethnically. Allow friendships to develop through the use of exercises in class-building, team-building, and cooperative learning. Then, introduce whatever competitive strategies seem appropriate for the situation.

CONCLUSION: THE ULTIMATE GOAL OF JIGSAW LEARNING

As we have said repeatedly (even harped on), the goal of cooperative learning is not to train young people to be so cooperative that they will be out of place in a highly competitive society. Rather, *the goal is to teach cooperation as a skill,* one that the individual can call on under appropriate conditions—when cooperation is the most appropriate and most useful way to perform a task—even in an environment that is largely competitive. And it is abundantly clear that this is a reasonable goal.

Our systematic research shows, over and over again, that youngsters can and do cooperate under appropriate conditions. Moreover, this same research demonstrates clearly that youngsters who have spent a year or more in a classroom where cooperation is the dominant mode of interaction perform as well as or better than they ever did when they have subsequently been moved to a classroom environment in which competition predominates. Our hope is that as a result of their jigsaw experience they have lost only one thing: their tendency to behave in the mindless manner described in the opening of this chapter and to compete blindly—to try to beat the other person in situations where cooperation would be a more appropriate strategy.

Beyond that, it is our hope that children who have experienced the pleasures as well as the benefits of cooperation in school might venture to try out cooperation as a strategy even in ambiguous situations. Most American youngsters, reared as they are on a fairly steady diet of competitiveness, seem to have one major strategy: when in doubt, go out there and win. For us, the ultimate goal is to help young people learn that cooperation can be appropriate, functional, and humanizing in many more situations than they might have realized. It is even conceivable that as more and more of today's youngsters develop skills in cooperation as part of their educational experience and as they move toward adulthood, the values of our society may begin to shift away from the relentless concern with winning. As we have seen, high standards and good performance are not necessarily incompatible with support, friendship, empathy, and a tolerance for individual differences. One can perform superlatively without doggedly striving to be number one.

A LETTER FROM CARLOS

Chapter 1 presented the story of Carlos, a Latino youngster who participated in the earliest research that I conducted with colleagues in Austin, Texas. The name "Carlos" was invented to protect the privacy of the youngster—but the child was a real person—not simply a composite made up of the experiences of four or five youngsters. Indeed, Carlos was so real and his individual experience so touching that, over the years, I have told his story in a great many pieces I have written. Carlos's story was (and still is) the clearest way I know of illustrating the jigsaw technique and how it works. Imagine my surprise and delight when, several years later, I received the following letter:

Dear Professor Aronson:

I am a senior at University. Today I got a letter admitting me to the Harvard Law School. This may not seem odd to you but, let me tell you something. I am the 6th of 7 children my parents had—and I am the only one who ever went to college, let alone graduate, or go to law school.

By now, you are probably wondering why this stranger is writing to you and bragging to you about his achievements. Actually, I'm not a stranger although we never met. You see, last year I was taking a course in social psychology and we were using a book you wrote called *The Social Animal,* and when I read about prejudice and jigsaw it all sounded very familiar—and then, I realized that I was in that very first class you ever did jigsaw in—when I was in the 5th grade. And as I read on, it dawned on me that I was the boy that you called Carlos. And then I remembered you when you first came to our classroom and how I was scared and how I hated school and how I was so stupid and didn't know anything. And you came in—it all came back to me when I read your book—you were very tall—about 6½ feet—and you had a big black beard and you were funny and made us all laugh.

And, most important, when we started to do work in jigsaw groups, I began to realize that I wasn't really that stupid. And the kids I thought were cruel and hostile became my friends and the teacher acted friendly and nice to me and I actually began to love school, and I began to love to learn things and now I'm about to go to Harvard Law School.

You must get a lot of letters like this but I decided to write anyway because let me tell you something. My mother tells me that when I was born I almost died. I was born at home and the cord was wrapped around my neck and the midwife gave me mouth to mouth and saved my life. If she was still alive, I would write to her too, to tell her that I grew up smart and good and I'm going to law school. But she died a few years ago. I'm writing to you because, no less than her, you saved my life too.

It is a beautiful letter—perhaps the most moving letter I have ever received. But when I read the signature I realized that it did not belong to the boy that I had in mind—the boy I called "Carlos." So I thought about that for a while, and then I fell into a kind of reverie and I allowed myself the luxury of beginning to think grandiose thoughts. Specifically, I began to imagine that, because of jigsaw, there were *thousands* of kids all over America who mistakenly think they are Carlos. And then I realized that perhaps it is I who am mistaken; in the deepest sense, of course, they all *are* Carlos!

Elliot Aronson

NASA EXERCISE: SEEKING CONSENSUS

Goals[1]
- To compare the results of individual decision making with the results of group decision making
- To diagnose the level of development in a task-oriented group

Group Size
- Between 6 and 12 participants; several groups may be directed simultaneously

Time Required
- Approximately 1 hour

Materials
- Pencils
- Individual work sheets
- Group work sheets
- Answer sheets containing rationale for decisions
- Direction sheets for scoring

Physical Setting
- Participants should be seated around a square or round table. The dynamics of a group seated at a rectangular table are such that it gives too much control to persons seated at the ends.

Process
- Participants are each given a copy of the individual work sheet and told that they have 15 fifteen minutes to complete the exercise.

[1] The NASA Exercise was invented by Dr. Jay Hall and is reprinted with his permission.

- One group work sheet is handed to each group.
- Individuals are *not* to change any answers on their individual sheets as a result of group discussion.
- A member of the group is to record group consensus on this sheet.
- The participants will have 30 minutes in which to complete the group work sheet.
- Each participant is given a copy of the direction sheet for scoring.

This phase of the experience should take 7 to 10 minutes.
- Participants score their individual work sheets.
- They will then give their score to the recorder, who will compute the average of the individual scores.
- The recorder scores the group work sheet.
- The group computes the average score for individuals with the group score and discusses the implications of the experience. This phase of the experience should take 7 to 10 minutes.
- Results are posted according to the chart below, and the facilitator directs a discussion of the outcomes of consensus seeking and the experience of negotiating agreement.

	Group 1	Group 2	Group 3
Consensus score			
Average score			
Range of individual scores			

NASA EXERCISE: INDIVIDUAL WORK SHEET AND GROUP WORK SHEET

INDIVIDUAL WORK SHEET

Instructions

You are a member of a space crew originally scheduled to rendezvous with a mother ship on the lighted surface of the moon. Due to mechanical difficulties, however, your ship is forced to land at a spot some 200 miles from the rendezvous point. During landing, much of the equipment aboard is damaged, and, since survival depends on reaching the mother ship, the most critical items available must be chosen for the 200-mile trip. Below are listed the 15 items left intact and undamaged after landing. Your task is to rank order them in terms of their importance to your crew in allowing them to reach the rendezvous point. Place the number 1 by the most important item, the number 2 by the second most important, and so on, through number 15, the least important. *You have 15 minutes to complete this phase of the exercise.*

GROUP WORK SHEET

Instructions

This is an exercise in group decision making. Your group is to employ the method of *Group Consensus* in reaching its decision. This means that the ranking of each of the 15 survival items *must* be agreed upon by each group member before it becomes a part of the group decision. Consensus is difficult to reach. Therefore not every ranking will meet with everyone's complete *approval*. Try as a group to make each ranking one with which *all* group members can at least partially agree. Here are some guides to use in reaching consensus:

- Avoid arguing for your own individual judgments. Approach the task on the basis of logic.
- Avoid changing your mind only in order to reach agreement and avoid conflict. Support only solutions with which you are able to agree somewhat at least.
- Avoid "conflict-reducing" techniques such as majority vote, averaging, or trading in reaching your decision.
- View differences of opinion as helpful rather than as a hindrance in decision-making.

Fifteen Items for Individual and Group Work Sheet

_____ Box of matches

_____ Food concentrate

_____ 50 feet of nylon rope

_____ Parachute silk

_____ Portable heating unit

_____ Two .45 caliber pistols

_____ One case dehydrated milk

_____ Two 100-1b. tanks of oxygen

_____ Stellar map (of moon's constellation)

_____ Life raft

_____ Magnetic compass

_____ 5 gallons of water

_____ Signal flares

_____ First-aid kit containing injection needles

_____ Solar-powered FM receiver-transmitter

APPENDIX C

ANSWER SHEET FOR NASA EXERCISE

Correct Rank		Rationale
15	Box of matches	No oxygen
4	Food concentrate	Can live for some time without food
6	50 feet of nylon rope	For travel over rough terrain
8	Parachute silk	Good for carrying items
13	Portable heating unit	Lighted side of moon is hot
11	Two .45 caliber pistols	Can be used for propulsion
12	One case dehydrated milk	Needs H_2O to work
1	Two 100-1b. tanks of oxygen	No air on moon
3	Stellar map (of moon's constellation)	Needed for navigation
9	Life raft	Some value for shelter or carrying
14	Magnetic compass	Moon's magnetic field is different from earth's
2	5 gallons of water	You can't live long without this
10	Signal flares	No oxygen
7	First-aid kit containing needles	First-aid kit might be needed but needles are useless
5	Solar-powered FM receiver-transmitter	Communication

DIRECTION SHEET FOR SCORING NASA EXERCISE

The group recorder will assume the responsibility for directing the scoring. Individuals will do the following:

1. Score the net difference between their answers and correct answers. For example, if the answer is 9, and the correct answer is 12, the net difference will be 3, the score for that particular item.
2. Total these scores for an individual score.
3. Total all individual scores and divide by the number of participants; this number represents the average of individual scores.
4. Score the net difference between group work sheet answers and the correct answers.

5. Total these scores for a group score.

6. Compare the average individual score with the group score.

RATINGS

0-20   Excellent

20-30   Good

30-40   Average

40-50   Fair

Over 50   Poor

REFERENCES

Aronson, E., Blaney, N., Sikes, J., Stephan, C, & Snapp, M. (1975). Busing and racial tension: The jigsaw route to learning and liking, *Psychology Today, 8,* 43-59.

Aronson, E., Blaney, N., & Stephan, C. (1975, September). *Cooperation in the classroom: The jigsaw puzzle model.* Paper presented at the annual meeting of the American Psychological Association, Chicago.

Aronson, E., Bridgeman, D., & Geffner, R. (1978). The effects of cooperative classroom structure on student behavior and attitudes. In D. Bar-Tal and L. Saxe (Eds.), *Social psychology of education.* Washington: Hemisphere.

Aronson, E., & Gonzalez, A. (1988). Desegregation, jigsaw and the Mexican-American experience. In P. Katz and D. Taylor, *Eliminating racism.* New York: Plenum.

Aronson, E., & Goode, E. (1980). Training teachers to implement jigsaw learning: A manual for teachers. In E. Sharan, R. Hare, C. Webb, & R. Hertz-Lazarowitz (Eds.). *Cooperation in education* (pp. 47-81). Provo: Brigham Young University Press.

Aronson, E., & Thibodeau, R. (1992). The jigsaw classroom: A cooperative strategy for reducing prejudice. In J. Lynch, C. Modgil, & S. Modgil, *Cultural diversity in the schools.* London: Falmer Press.

Bavelas, A. (1973). The five squares problem: an instructional aid in group cooperation, *Studies in Personnel Psychology, 5,* 29-38.

Blaney, N., Stephan, C., Rosenfield, D., Aronson, E., & Sikes, J. (1977). Interdependence in the classroom: A field study, *Journal of Educational Psychology, 69,* 121-128.

Bridgeman, D. L. (1977). *The influence of cooperative, interdependent learning on role taking and moral reasoning: A theoretical and empirical field study with fifth-grade students.* Unpublished doctoral dissertation, University of California, Santa Cruz.

Bridgeman, D. (1981). Enhanced role-taking through cooperative interdependence: A field study, *Child Development, 52,* 1231-1238.

Brookover, W. B., Patterson, A., & Thomas, S. (1964). Self-concept of ability and school achievement, *Sociology of Education, 37,* 271-278.

Chandler, M. J. (1973). Egocentrism and antisocial behavior: The assessment and training of social perspective-taking skills, *Developmental Psychology, 9,* 326-332.

Clark, J., Wideman, R., & Eadie, S. (1990). *Together We Learn.* Scarborough, Ontario: Prentice-Hall Canada.

Cloward, R. (1967). Studies in tutoring, *Journal of Experimental Education, 36,* 14-25.
Coelho, E., Winer, L., & Olson, J. W. (1989). *All sides of the issue: Activities/or cooperative jigsaw groups.* Hayward, CA: Alemany Press.

Cohen, E. (1986). *Designing group work: Strategies for the heterogeneous classroom.* New York: Teachers College Press.

Coleman, J. S. (1966). *Equality of educational opportunity.* Washington: Department of Health, Education, and Welfare.

Courtis, S., McSwain, E., & Morrison, N. (1937). *Teachers and cooperation.* Washington: National Education Association.

Covington, M. V., & Beery, R. G. (1976). *Self-worth and school learning.* New York: Holt, Rinehart, and Winston.

Deutsch, M. (1949). A theory of cooperation and competition. *Human Relations, 2,* 129-152.

DeVries, D. L. (1977, August). Teams-games-tournament: Five years of research. Paper presented at the annual meeting of the American Psychological Association, San Francisco.

Dishon, D., & O'Leary, P. W. (1984). *A guidebook for cooperative learning: A technique for creating more effective schools.* Holmes Beach, FL: Learning Publications.

Franks, D. D., & Marolla, J. (1976). Efficacious action and social approval as interacting dimensions of self-esteem: A tentative formulation through construct validation, *Sociometry, 39*, 324-341.

Foyie, H. C, Lyman, L., & Thies, A. (1991). *Cooperative learning in the early childhood classroom.* Washington: National Education Association.

Gaertner, S. L., Mann, J. A., Dovidio, J. F, Murrell, A. J., & Pomare, M. (1990). How does cooperation reduce intergroup bias? *Journal of Personality and Social Psychology, 59*, 692-704.

Garibaldi, A. (1977, August). Cooperation, competition, individualization, and black students' problem solving and attitudes. Paper presented at the annual meeting of the American Psychological Association, San Francisco.

Geffner, R. A. (1978). *The effects of interdependent learning on self-esteem, interethnic relations, and intraethnic attitudes of elementary school children: A field experiment.* Unpublished doctoral dissertation, University of California, Santa Cruz.

Gerard, H., & Miller, N. (1975). *School desegregation.* New York: Plenum Press. Gibbs, J. (1987). *Tribes: A process for social development and cooperative learning.* Santa Rosa, CA: Center Source Publications.

Graves, N., & Graves, T. (Eds.). (1987). *Cooperative learning: A resource guide.* Santa Cruz, CA. Haines, D. B., & McKeachie, W. J. (1967). Cooperative versus competitive discussion methods in teaching introductory psychology, *Journal of Educational Psychology, 58*, 386-390.

Heider, F. (1958). *The psychology of interpersonal relations.* New York: Wiley.

Hertz-Lazarowitz, R., Benveniste-Kirkus, V, & Miller, N. (1992). Implications of current research on cooperative interaction for classroom application. In R. Hertz-Lazarovitz & N. Miller (Eds.), *Interaction in cooperative groups. The theoretical anatomy of group learning* (pp. 235-280). Cambridge: Cambridge University Press.

Holt, J. (1967). *How children learn.* New York: Dell.

Johnson, D. W., & Johnson, R. (1977, August). *Cooperation, competition, and individualization and interracial, intersexual, and interability attitudes.* Paper presented at the annual meeting of the American Psychological Association, San Francisco.

Johnson, D. W., & Johnson, R. (1989). *Cooperation and Competition: Theory and Research.* Edina, MN: Interaction.

Johnson, D. W., Johnson, R., & Maruyama, G. (1981). Interdependence and interpersonal attraction among heterogeneous individuals: A theoretical formulation and a meta-analysis of the research, *Review of Educational Research, 53*, 5-54.

Johnson, D. W., Johnson, R., Holubec, E., & Roy, P. (1990). *Circles of Learning: Cooperation in the Classroom* (3rd ed.). Edina, MN: Interaction.

Johnson, D., Johnson, R., & Scott, R. (1991). *Learning together and alone: Cooperative, competitive, and individualistic learning* (3rd ed.). Boston: Allyn and Bacon.

Jones, E. E., & Davis, K. E. (1965). From acts to dispositions. In L. Berkowitz (Ed.), *Advances in experimental social psychology* (Vol. 2.). New York: Academic Press.

Kagan, S. (1992). *Cooperative learning.* San Juan Capistrano, CA.: Kagan Cooperative Learning.

Kagan, S. (1985). Dimensions of cooperative classroom structures. In R. Slavin, S.

Sharan, S. Kagan, R. Hertz-Lazarowitz, C. Webb, & R. Schmuck (Eds.), *Learning to cooperate, cooperating to learn* (pp. 67-96). New York: Plenum.

Kagan, S., & Madsen, M. C. (1971). Cooperation and competition of Mexican, Mexican American, and Anglo-American children of two ages under four instructional sets, *Developmental Psychology, 5,* 32-39.

Kohn, A. (1986). *No contest.* Boston: Houghton Mifflin. Lippitt, P., Eiseman, J., & Lippitt, R. (1969). *Cross-age helping program: Orientation, training, and related materials.* Ann Arbor: University of Michigan, Center for Research on Utilization of Scientific Knowledge, Institute for Social Research.

Lippitt, P., & Lohman, J. (1965). Cross-age relationships—an educational resource. *Children, 12,* 113-117.

Lucker, G. W., Rosenfield, D., Sikes, J., & Aronson, E. (1977). Performance in the interdependent classroom: A field study, *American Educational Research Review, 13,* 115-123.

Lyman, L., Foyle, H. C, & Azwell, T. S. (1993). *Cooperative learning in the elementary classroom.* Washington: National Education Association.

Madsen, M. C. (1967). Cooperative and competitive motivation of children in three Mexican subcultures, *Psychological Reports, 20,* 1307-1320.

Madsen, M. C. (1971). Developmental and cross-cultural differences in cooperative and competitive behavior of young children, *Journal of Cross-Cultural Psychology, 2,* 365-371.

Madsden, M. C, and Shapira, A. (1970). Cooperative and competitive behavior of urban Afro-American, Anglo-American, Mexican-American, and Mexican village children, *Developmental Psychology, 3,* 16-20.

Maruyama, G. (1991). Meta-analyses relating goal structures to achievement: Findings, controversies, and impacts, *Personality and Social Psychology Bulletin, 17(3),* 300-305.

McConahay, J. B. (1981). Reducing racial prejudice in desegregated schools. In W. D. Hawley (Ed.), *Effective school desegregation.* Beverly Hills: Sage.

Nelson, L. L., & Kagan, S. (1972, September). Competition: The starspangled scramble, *Psychology Today,* p. 53.

Phillips, B. N., & D'Amico, L. A. (1956). Effects of cooperation and competition on the cohesiveness of small face-to-face groups, *Journal of Educational Psychology, 47,* 65-70.

Postman, N., & Weingartner, C. (1969). *Teaching as a subversive activity.* New York: Delta.

Purkey, W. W. (1970). *Self-concept and school achievement.* Englewood Cliffs, NJ: Prentice-Hall.

Schmuck, R. A., & Schmuck, P. A. (1983). *Group processes in the classroom.* Dubuque, IA: William C. Brown.

Sharan, S. (Ed.). (1990). *Cooperative learning: Theory and research.* New York: Praeger. Sharan, S., & Hertz-Lazarowitz, R. (1982). Effects of an instructional change program on teachers' behavior, attitudes, and perceptions, *Journal of Applied Behavioral Science, 18,* 85-201.

Sharan, Y., & Sharan, S. (1992). *Expanding cooperative learning through group investigation.* New York: Teachers College Press.

Slavin, R. (1990). *Cooperative learning: Theory, research, and practice.* Boston: Allyn and Bacon.

Slavin, R. (1977, August). Student teams and peer tutoring. Paper presented at the annual meeting of the American Psychological Association, San Francisco.

Slavin, R. (1977). Student team-learning techniques: Narrowing the gap between the races (Report No. 228, Center for Social Organization of Schools). Baltimore: Johns Hopkins University.

Slavin, R. (1983a). *Cooperative learning.* New York: Longman.

Slavin, R. (1983b). When does cooperative learning increase student achievement? *Psychological Bulletin, 94,* 429-445.

Slavin, R. (1991). *Student team learning: A practical guide to cooperative learning* (3rd ed.). Washington: National Education Association.

Slavin, R., Sharan, S., Kagan, S., Hertz-Lazarowitz, R., Webb, C, & Schmuck, R. (Eds.). (1985). *Learning to cooperate, cooperating to learn.* New York: Plenum.

Stendler, C, Damrin, D., &; Haines, A. C. (1951). Studies in cooperation and competition: 1. The effects of working for group and individual rewards on the social climate of children's groups, *Journal of Genetic Psychology, 79,* 173-197.

Stephan, C, Kennedy, J. C, & Aronson, E. (1977). The effects of friendship and outcome on task attribution, *Sociometry, 40,* 107-111.

Stephan, W. (1978). School desegregation: An evaluation of predictions made in Brown v. the Board of Education, *Psychological Bulletin, 85,* 217-238.

Weigel, R. H., Wiser, P. L., & Cook, S. W. (1975). The impact of cooperative learning experiences on cross-ethnic relations and attitudes, *Journal of Social Issues, 31,* 219-244.

BOOKS BY ELLIOT ARONSON

Theories of cognitive consistency (with R. Abelson and others). Chicago: Rand McNally, 1968.

Voices of modern psychology. Reading, MA: Addison-Wesley, 1969. *Social psychology* (with R. Helmreich). New York: Van Nostrand, 1973.

The jigsaw classroom. Beverly Hills: Sage, 1978.

Burnout: From tedium to personal growth (with A. Pines & D. Kafry). New York: Free Press, 1981.

Energy use: The human dimension (with P. C. Stern). New York: W. H. Freeman, 1984.

The handbook of social psychology (2nd ed., with G. Lindzey). Reading, MA: Addison-Wesley, 1968-1969; (3rd ed. with G. Lindzey), New York: Random House, 1985.

Career burnout (with A. Pines). New York: Free Press, 1988.

Methods of research in social psychology (2nd ed., with P. Ellsworth, M. Carslmith, & M. Gonzales,). New York: Random House, 1990.

Age of propaganda (with A. R. Pratkanis). New York: W. H. Freeman, 1992.

Social psychology (3 vols., with A. R. Pratkanis). London: Elgar, 1992.

Social psychology: The heart and the mind (with T. Wilson & R. Akert). New York: HarperCollins, 1994.

Readings about the social animal (7th ed.). New York: W. H. Freeman, 1995.

The social animal (7th ed.). New York: W. H. Freeman, 1995.

Mistakes were made (but not by me) (with C. Tavris). New York: Harcourt, 2007.

Not by chance alone: my life as a social psychologist. New York: Basic Books, 2010.

INDEX

busing and, 6-7
and competition, 5
social psychology of, 6-8
Deutsch, Morton, 18
DeVries, David, 108

Empathy, 26, 88-89, 109
Expert group(s), 42-44
leadership of, 43-44
and reading problems, 62
teacher intervention and, 53-54

Facilitator, teacher's role as, 45-46
Fish-bowling, 97-99, 101
Franks, David, 85

Gaertner, Samuel, 88
Garibaldi, Antoine, 107
Geffner, Robert, 84
Gerard, Harold, 6
Group(s)
expert. *See* Expert group(s)
goals of, 21
and group investigation, 18, 22
and group picture, 28
and intergroup competition, 35-36
intervention in. *See* Intervention
jigsaw. *See* Jigsaw group(s)
leaders of. *See* Group leader(s)
Group goals, 21
Group investigation, 18, 22
Group leader(s)
of expert group, 43-44
intervention by, 50-51
selection of, 48
student, 46-47
training of, 48-52
Group picture, 28
Group process sheet, 35-36
illustrated, 36

Heads together, 16
Heider, Fritz, 85
Helping skills, 27-34
Hispanic children, 13, 82, 84, 88. *See also* Carlos
Holt, John, 26
Individual accountability, 21

Inner self-esteem, 85
In-service workshop. *See* Jigsaw workshop
Instructional materials. *See also* Curriculum
alternative, 60
obtaining and developing, 64-65
sharing of, 64-65
Interdependence, 10, 23, 40
Intergroup competition, 35-36
Intervention
by group leader, 50-51
by teacher, 53-54
"I" statements, 58-59

Jigsaw. *See also* Jigsaw classroom
and absenteeism, 13, 82
and academic performance, 12-13, 19, 20, 87-88
and Austin project, 7-13, 74, 88, 111
basic results of, 12-14
and Carlos case study, 11-14
and cooperative learning strategies, 22-23. *See also* Cooperative learning
curriculum and, 39-42
and empathy for others, 26, 88-89, 109
goal of, 13, 106, 109-110
group for. *See* Jigsaw group(s)
how it works, 53-54
and jigsaw cards, 40-42
and learning from others, 87
origins of, 5
problems in, 55-68
research on. *See* Jigsaw research
sharing of. *See* Jigsaw workshop
and source of name, 9
special roles in, 45-48
students and, 38-39
subject matter adapted for, 9n, 39-42
and teacher as facilitator, 45-46
Jigsaw cards, 40-42
Jigsaw classroom, 8-11
academic performance in, 12-13, 19-20, 87-88
and African-American children, 6, 13, 82, 84, 88, 104
analysis of, 73
competition in, 87, 107-109
cooperative spirit in, 66-67